THE SECRET PLACE, REVEALED

THE CREATED, ALONE WITH THE CREATOR

KEVIN KINCHEN

THE SECRET PLACE, REVEALED
THE CREATED, ALONE WITH THE CREATOR

Published by:
Kingdom House
P.O. Box 2825
Peoria, Arizona 85380

ISBN 978-0-615-44149-8

DEDICATION

First, I have to dedicate this book to the Master of all, Jesus Christ. Without Him, I am nothing; with Him, there are no limits. I am grateful He chose me as one of His representatives. What an honor and privilege it is to serve Him. Thank You, Jesus!

Second, I dedicate this book to my wife, Margie, and my kids, Jared, Josh, and Courtney; including my daughters-in-law Rachel and Lauren, and grandsons, Kallan, Kooper, and Jett. Without all of you, life would be extremely boring. You always manage to keep me laughing, sometimes embarrassed, but laughing. Margie, I am alive because you and Jesus are the ultimate life givers. You have prayed me out of death's grip more than once. You are true to your calling of "making me great." Words are not enough to show my appreciation, but I say, "thank you" anyway. You have put up with a lot and I know your reward in heaven will be HUGE. I love you more today than ever! Kids, all of you; thanks for allowing me to pursue and fulfill the call of God on my life. I know you have had to share me with the world. God knows and He says, "thank you." I am stinkin' proud of all of you and I love you too!

Third, I dedicate this book to two people who have invested a lifetime into me, Pastors Al and Judy Jandl, my pastors for almost thirty years. Your wisdom, time, discipleship, discipline, finances, forgiveness, encouragement, prayers, leadership, and friendship are without a doubt, a huge part of who I am today. I am forever grateful for both of you believing in me when I was not even sure I believed in myself. Face it, I'm your son and you cannot get rid of me! I love you both!

Last, but certainly not least, I dedicate this book to my biggest fan, my mom. Thanks for everything, Mom! From the braces to the speech therapy to buying every message I preach, you are awesome! I love you like crazy!

ACKNOWLEDGEMENTS

So many people have played a vital role in this book becoming a reality. There is no way I could name all of you, but trust me, God knows and so do Margie and I. I have to THANK all the wonderful E-quippers and Partners who believe in our ministry, pray for us, and invest in us all the time. Together, we really are making a difference. I pray God will bless all of you for your faithfulness! And remember, this is only the beginning!

A special Thank You to:

• Jim and Kathy McKimmy—You guys are the best of the best! Thank you both for all you do for us. We are so glad God hooked the four of us together. I pray it stays that way forever! The seeds you sow into us are producing an exponential harvest. I know God smiles when He sees you. And frankly, Margie and I crack up laughing too! Both of you are, *"Wonderful human beings!"*

• Paul and Dana Treadgold—Thank you for investing in what appeared to be an invisible book. Whew, it's finally done and you both are a big part of it. Over the years, you have sown many seeds into us. I pray this book gives you a glimpse of your reward. Thanks for everything!

• My terrific yet tough (Just kidding.) editors—Amy Jo Secker, Shana Anderson, Richard Albritton, and Margie. You guys are so smart it's scary. The readers thank you for your hard work, and so do I. Or, is it, "I thank you and so do the readers…" Oh well, you get my point. I love all of you!

- James Pitkin—You are the most creative being I have ever met. This book cover you designed is absolutely stunning! You always amaze me and you are so good to me. Thank you for everything. Get ready for more book covers!

- J.H. Photography—What can I say? You make me look good! And you did it without Photoshop… at least I think you did. If not, don't tell me. Thanks for capturing everything I envisioned with your camera!

TABLE OF CONTENTS

FOREWORD

By: Pastor Al Jandl

There are several books written about the "Secret Place" but those birthed from experience have a life-changing effect on the reader. In his writings, Kevin will introduce you to a walk of trusting God in all types of situations and circumstances. To say his walk has been without discouragement and suffering would not show the real picture of his life. Instead you will find a strong devotion for his God that always led him to the "Secret Place."

Prayer has always been a central vein in Kevin's life. For many years he rose around 5 a.m. to spend his time with God before our work day started at the Church. Not only did I appreciate his faithfulness to me as his Pastor, but I admired his devotion to spiritual matters. One day a tragedy struck when a backhoe ran over the full length of his body, and as I cried out to God for his life, God spoke Psalm 91:14 -16 to me. *"Because he hath set his love upon me, therefore will I deliver him: I will set him on high because he hath known my name. He shall call upon me, and I will answer him; I will be with him in trouble; I will deliver him, and honor him. With long life will I satisfy him, and shew him my salvation."* Through the years I have personally witnessed Kevin's love for God and his sincere desire to be in His presence, I have also seen the many times God has delivered him.

Kevin, and his wife Margie, have been an active part of our church for thirty years. I have watched him grow spiritually as he has served our church and served his Pastors, while on staff and even now as he evangelizes. He has displayed characteristics like loyalty, faithfulness, and the honoring of authority. Through the best of times and worst of times Kevin has been faithful to give God, our church, and his family 100 percent. I have also witnessed the inward transformation shown by the peace of God and the joy of the Lord that shines from Kevin. That is the true evidence of the time he has spent in "The Secret Place."

INTRODUCTION

Whenever we experience something great, we tell other people. Whenever we experience something life-changing we tell everyone. Whenever we experience something great AND life-changing, AND we experience it over and over and over again, we write a book about it and hope everyone reads it. That's why I am writing this book.

A good number of years ago I was a frustrated, confused, unfulfilled, and directionless person... all while being in full-time ministry! I had become a Christian through a miraculous series of events as a senior in high school and watched as God transformed my life in a very short period. I became sold out to do whatever God had planned for me and I didn't care how He used me, as long as He used me. God was faithful and He was certainly working through me. Things changed though. After several years of ministry as a senior pastor, I found myself wanting to find my "niche" I was created to fulfill. It wasn't enough to be "busy" for God. I had to know why I was created and what I was put on the earth to do... specifically.

After years of struggles, disappointments, dead-end pursuits, and detours, I found what I had needed all along. You see, what started out as a great relationship with God had turned into a working relationship with God. My passion to know the Lord had somehow turned into a passion to do things for Him. Wow, did I ever make a crazy mess out of everything.

Thankfully, God had many divine appointments, revelations, and people that would work their way into my life to help me get things back in order. I found my first love again, and the REALationship He desired for me. I found the Secret Place; that place where we get alone with the One who created us. It's in the Secret Place where we can find anything and everything we will ever need or desire. It's where we get close to God and begin to see what He has for us instead of what we have for ourselves.

That is what this book is all about. It's about the created learning how to get alone with the Creator. It reveals the difference between knowing God and knowing "about" Him. I wrote this book based on Scripture and on what I have experienced over almost three decades. My time in the Secret Place is something I have tested, proven, lived, and developed in and through my life. After twenty-six years of ministry, I have seen others embrace it and experience results in their own lives as well.

While in Romania in 2009, my wife and I met a college student named Alexandra. I spoke at her church's Sunday service and also to their college group. When I spoke to the students, I shared a quick version of what getting alone with God has done in my life. I also shared about the Secret Place. The whole message was maybe fifteen to twenty minutes long. A seed had been planted. I received a letter recently from Alexandra that shows what God can do with only a little seed of His Word. Here is Alexandra's letter.

Dearest Kevin,

I thank the Lord for the awesome breakthrough I had in my heart, this year... He said: *learn to be still and you will know that I am your Lord...* I did practice that... till one day He took me beyond the veil, in a secret place where I could call "my hiding place," "my refuge" in times of trouble, a place where only worship and thanksgiving could come along with me, a place of healing and deliverance, a place where I become one in Him and He in me, a place where the bride meets the groom and touches the love, kindness and tenderness that He has for her, the Holy of Holies, His sanctuary inside me, ... a place where He released the "joy of my salvation" to my heart and I will never be the same person, again.

I know Him personally now, and we are bound with intimate-cords that cannot be broken. Revealing that place inside of me... has brought inner transformation and will continue... from glory to glory... till the **fullness** of the Lord is being manifested in me, and through me to others. Amen!

Thank you Jesus!

Thank you Pastor Kevin!

Alexandra

Wow! What an incredible testimony! If God will do that for Alexandra, then He will do it for you. I believe you are holding this book in your hand for a reason. It's a divine appointment that is bigger than you or me. Get ready for "His sanctuary inside you" to totally transform your life.

My desire is for people to see Jesus inside of me. I want to be able to make the bold statement the apostle Paul made when he said, *"Follow my example, as I follow the example of Christ" (1 Cor. 11:1 New International Version)*. I believe the Secret Place creates such an atmosphere for this to happen.

I pray this book is a blessing to you. I also pray that the Holy Spirit will share life-changing truths with you as He has done for me. As you read, take the time, to make the time, to spend some time with God. Time is essential in any relationship, and it's vital for a REALationship. As you will soon learn, this REALationship with God in the Secret Place will have extraordinary results in YOUR life and in the lives of everyone you meet or know.

Make sure you read this book all the way to the end. And by all means, don't let the Secret Place continue to be a secret... the Secret Place has been REVEALED!

CHAPTER I

Run Over By A 13,000 lb Tractor; LENGTHWISE!

The Secret Place, Revealed. Nice title, but what's it about? Well, the Secret Place has been around forever. From Adam to the apostle Paul, people had many seasons and times alone with God. Moses almost wore out a path up the mountain because of all his meetings with God. He may have called it "mountain time" instead of the Secret Place. Enoch had such great fellowship with God that one day he never came back; He was "taken." (Gen. 5:24) He must have experienced the presence of God in an incredible way that moved him into heaven before his time!

Jesus certainly had a record of alone time with His Father. Early morning and the middle of the night seemed to be his favorite times. He also had a thing for mountains like Moses. The saints of Old tell of times with God. Maybe they were times of prayer or fasting but they definitely had time alone with God. All throughout the history of mankind this special time with the Lord has been practiced.

So, what is it about the Secret Place that inspired me to write a book about it? In my own personal life, I have experienced many great things during my time alone with God. I am talking about life altering things, not simple goose bumps and emotions. In fact, I am talking about life itself. Beyond my spiritual life, my actual physical life is a result of time in the Secret Place. Let me share what I mean by that.

In 1993, I was the camp director at Victory Camp in Alvin, Texas. On July 5, a group of us gathered for a workday to tear down a building and do some major clean up. At about 11:30 in the morning, one of the volunteers radioed to tell me our old CASE 580 backhoe would not start. This was typical so we grabbed some jumper cables and proceeded to get it going.

I had been around tractors for many years and had even owned a tractor business with my brother for a time. I was comfortable working on and around them, so I quickly hooked the cables up for a routine jump-start. There was no clue that within the next sixty seconds my life would literally be hanging by the thread of a prayer... and nothing else.

I was standing between the back wheel and front wheel while trying to jump-start the backhoe. As I reached through the hydraulic hoses to turn the key on, the tractor started and lunged forward, running over me from feet to head with my face up. I was in too big of a hurry and had forgotten to make sure the backhoe was in neutral. As it ran over me, its weight of approximately 13,000 pounds felt more like a million pounds. The back wheel that ran over my body lengthwise stood about chest high and was almost as wide as me. The workday was over for me but the fight for my life had begun.

My first thought was, "My eyes have been totally rearranged on my forehead because everything is cross-eyed!" I could not focus on anything at all. I began to notice a tremendous amount of "warm stuff" coming out of my mouth. Minutes later, I realized each mouthful was the warmth of my own blood.

That is when the fear hit me. The thought of losing that much blood made me realize this was a major accident and I may not recover. Thoughts of dying and the struggle to breathe were coupled together in a fear I had never experienced.

The pain of a crushed body

The immediate pain I felt as the backhoe ran over me was that of a severe blow to my head. It was as if someone had hit me square in the face with 100 baseball bats. The pain of the impact was beyond description. I don't remember feeling any pain from the gash in my wrist or from the eleven broken ribs. All I remember is the panic that triggered every time I gasped to take a breath of air. I felt as though I was drowning and suffocating all at the same time. Of course, later I discovered this was due to my lungs filling up with fluid and the crush injury to my chest.

All this was happening within a matter of minutes or even seconds. I know I must have been in shock because they said I stood up and turned in a circle before I collapsed to the ground. I don't remember that at all. Why would anyone attempt to get up after they were run over? Obviously, the body and the mind can do some weird things when run over by 13,000 pounds.

Utter confusion, that's what seemed to be running through my mind. I could not figure out how I had been hurt so badly in a matter of seconds. All I was doing was jump-starting a tractor. I had done it many times before with no incident. All of a sudden I was gasping for breath, coughing up blood, and wondering if my life was about to be over. It wasn't until after I had been in the hospital for a few days that I finally pieced the accident together and realized what had happened.

Family and friends... priceless

I thank God I was not alone that day. It was a volunteer workday and there were a number of people helping at the camp. My wife, Margie, and our kids were on site helping as well. My son Josh, who was eight years old at the time, was standing right beside me when I reached over to start the backhoe. It's only by the grace of God that he was not in the way of the backhoe as it plowed over my body.

I remember the looks on some of my friends' faces while lying there, struggling to breathe. The looks spoke for themselves; it wasn't good. They were all praying and offering words of comfort in the best way they knew how. Several people grabbed a piece of plywood and held it over me to shield the hot Texas sun.

At that moment, it meant so much to me that believers were surrounding me physically and spiritually. As the news spread of the accident, people took care of our kids, they held Margie as she ran upon the scene, and even caught the run away backhoe after it had done its damage. They all continued to pray and speak the Word of God over me. I was certainly not alone that day. Even as I lost the ability to focus on those caring for me, I still felt that ultimate "Someone" on the inside. That Someone was Jesus.

After the initial blow by that back wheel, I knew I was hurt in a bad way but did my best not to think about death.

I usually have a positive outlook on things. Nevertheless, as things progressed, even my positive attitude became weak and doubtful. As the clock ticked and people told me that a Life Flight helicopter was on its way, I began to wonder if they would arrive in time. How could someone be losing massive amounts of blood and live? Those were the thoughts that were bombarding me.

Peace beyond comprehension and love without measure

Riding on the Life Flight helicopter was an experience within itself. During the flight, out of nowhere, I felt a peace come over me that I had never felt before and have never felt since. I remember thinking to myself, "This is it, I am about to breathe my last breath and I will be in heaven." My dad had passed away a few years before, and I thought for sure I was about to see him face to face once again. That peace far surpassed any of the pain I was feeling. The trauma, the panic, the fear, the desire to have breath, all disappeared. I knew I was on the edge of heaven about to meet Jesus.

JUST THEN I heard the cry of my eight-year-old son who was screaming as he saw the backhoe running over me. Remember, Josh had been standing right beside me when the accident happened. He was screaming, "Somebody help my daddy! Somebody help my daddy!" It was at that moment I realized I could not go to heaven yet. I had to live, live for Josh's sake. I had to live so he could see that the God I told him about, the God I preached about was and is a good God. I

19

simply could not allow myself to slip into the next life leaving him traumatized by this horrific accident.

It's amazing what "the love of a father" will do for his children. I was willing and even wanting to give up the heavenly peace I was feeling in order to save my son's future. This must have been how it was when God sent Jesus to the earth on behalf of our future. Jesus surely felt this same feeling when He left the comforts and benefits of heaven to save you and me in this traumatic world we live in.

The damage assessment, the experience, and a miracle

The nurses on the Life Flight helicopter must have knocked me out because I don't remember arriving at the hospital. In fact, I don't remember much of the thirteen-day hospital stay at all. They had me heavily sedated due to the pain my body was experiencing. I DO know it was not a comforting thought when I realized I was on a breathing machine and had six tubes inserted into both sides of my chest. I'm sure I thought, "This doesn't look good."

And it wasn't good. The pain was intense and the results were life-threatening for sure. I had eleven broken ribs, two punctured lungs, a ruptured spleen, a torn liver, a torn ACL in my knee, a gash in my wrist, a possible skull fracture, infections, and what would eventually be determined, a broken leg. No words could ever describe all that happened on what I thought would be a trouble free workday.

Margie tells me that people came in and prayed for me all the time. She would only allow certain people, though. She would not allow even one negative thing said in my hospital room. Since it was a life or death matter, she felt she could only allow those who would create an atmosphere of faith. She and others were constantly speaking God's Word over my life as well.

Our youth group even made a recording of themselves as they read Scriptures. Margie would put headphones on me and let it play over and over again. She wanted me to hear the Word of God and hear it from familiar voices. Somehow, I remember hearing those kids reading me Scriptures. Even when our bodies are fighting for life, our spirits are wide-awake and taking in the words of others. Thankfully, people were speaking words of life to me.

My brother, Kendall, came to the hospital and asked me why I was chasing a moving tractor? Being on a ventilator and having tubes down my throat, I motioned for a pen and paper. I drew him a picture of what had happened. I wanted him to know I was not stupid enough to chase a tractor... just stupid enough to try to start it while standing between the two wheels! You know, give me a little credit, right?

After thirteen days in the hospital, the doctors released me to go home, quite miraculous seeing as how they only gave me a 10 to 15 percent chance of survival. They told Margie if I lived, I might not be in "my right mind." That one is still up for debate but at least I lived, right? I actually went to church on that fourteenth day and walked up the steps to our podium (unassisted I might add) to give God glory for what

HE had done. Surprising, as it may seem, there was actually no rehabilitation given to me whatsoever. God is so good!

The value of a Godly wife

You have to realize, I was pretty much out of it with all the pain medications the doctors had me on for the majority of my hospital stay. Nevertheless, Margie was fully aware and constantly being reminded of my condition. With all this, she was still able to look at me and look to the Lord knowing He was big enough. I am telling those of you reading this book right now... it pays to be married to a Godly spouse. In fact, it may be what saves your life someday. It's certainly true for me!

I remember on the way home, as my mother and Margie drove me, looking out the window at a cloud free beautiful blue sky. I began to weep like a baby. Margie said, "What's wrong? Are you in pain?" I replied, "No, it's just that I didn't know if I would ever see another blue sky again!" When you are knocking at death's door, and live to tell about it, you sure change your outlook on life. It makes you realize what is truly important and what's not. I have never been the same since that day.

We arrived at home, but I was moving slowly. With the broken ribs, the torn ACL in my left knee and an incision from just under my breast bone to below my navel, I was moving slowly, but I lived. I was home with my family. I could continue with God's calling and show my children, along with the whole world, that God is big enough to do great miracles. And He is good enough that He did it for ME. I am totally convinced that what He has done for me, He will do for you. Are YOU convinced? I pray you are.

Miracle confirmed

I thank God for every single medical person who worked on me during this accident. From the ambulance crew, to the Life Flight crew, to the surgeons, nurses, and specialists, it was obvious God had already prepared who and what I needed. That's what the Bible means when it says, *"He knows what we have need of before we even ask"* *(Matt. 6:8)*. Even the medical team at UTMB hospital said it was miraculous. In fact, the chief administrator of the hospital came to see me right before they discharged me and said, "Kevin, this whole thing has been quite the miracle hasn't it?" Of course, I agreed.

Later, I found out just how much of a miracle it really was. One of the ambulance technicians and one of the Life Flight nurses were each members of our church. They both recognized me and began to pray for me the second they were on the scene. Coincidence? No, divine appointment!

An emergency room trauma doctor, from New York City, was in the first week of his new job at UTMB the day I arrived. As the helicopter brought me in, the chief of surgery told them to do a CT scan to see how bad the situation was. With no seniority and no authority, this trauma doctor told the chief surgeon, "If you take him for a CT scan he will die on the table. Get him to surgery now... he is dying." The surgeon not only listened but also followed his instructions. This turned out to be the right thing to do. How do I know all this? That New

York doctor came to see me and told me he was a Christian. He told me God had sent him all the way to Texas to be a part of saving my life. Once again, a coincidence? Not at all... MIRACULOUS!

No, God was NOT trying to teach me something

Often people seem to think a tragic accident like this comes from God Himself. They say He is trying to "teach you something." Well, I think if God wanted to "teach me something" He certainly could have found a better way than to squish me like a grape, don't you? Come on, would any of us teach our kids something by running them into the ground? Of course not! We are made in the image and the likeness of God. (Gen. 1:26) Yes, maybe we became sinful, but we are formed in His likeness. If I would not do that to my child, then I am confident God would not do it either. We learn lessons in the midst of things like this but it does not mean God caused the accident.

The truth is I am the one who did something stupid. A person should never start a piece of machinery while standing beside it. I knew better but was in a hurry and just wasn't thinking. I can't even blame the devil on this one. It was my own hand that turned the key that day, no one else. I do believe the enemy wanted to use it for his benefit. If he could take a preacher out with a backhoe, I am sure he would jump at the opportunity. However, the good God I have been telling you about is so good that He took a tragedy and turned it into a triumph. Once again, a good God is the kind of God you and I serve.

When God takes something bad and turns it into something good, He really knows what He is doing. This accident may have been traumatic, but when God turned it around, I felt like the apostle Paul in 2 Corinthians 1:9 where he says, *"In fact, we expected to die. But as a result, we stopped relying on ourselves and learned to rely only on God, who raises the dead."* Even though I was a sold-out believer before the accident, I still didn't realize the frailty of life. Since this accident, I appreciate things like "breathing." I appreciate my family more than ever. I have a passion to tell others about this personal, miracle-working, love filled God that rescued me from death.

I also realized the incredible effort we put into temporary things. If put into proper perspective, these "things" don't really matter at all. The main thing that happened to me after the accident was a full-blown realization of what Christianity really is. It's all about a relationship with God. I say it like this: a REALationship with God. When it's all said and done, that REALationship is all that matters. I'm not talking about just a social or pretend relationship, but a REAL one. I pray the Lord reveals this to you as He did to me, of course without having a tragedy as the catalyst for that revelation.

My place in the Secret Place

What does all this have to do with the Secret Place? I was sooooooooo thankful I had been in the Secret Place the morning of the accident. Many people never meet Jesus until a tragedy happens. That is not the preferred time to meet Him, if you ask me. (Not that any time is a bad time to meet Him, of course.)

I am so glad I knew Him BEFORE the accident. My intimate relationship with God is what gave me hope in this crucial time of my life. That place of intimacy with God is what the Secret Place is all about.

Psalms 91:12-14 says that when I call on Him, He will rescue me. I already knew this and began to remind myself of His promise. That morning, before anyone else showed up for the workday, I was in the sanctuary by myself. It was me and God... alone. That time with Him is something no amount of money could ever purchase. It's priceless. That time with Him was the "well" I would have to draw from just a few hours later. I didn't earn His presence, nor did I earn His healing by being alone with Him. I just experienced Him.

That fresh experience, that fresh almost tangible time with Him, was a deposit I could withdraw from in my desperate time of need. This presence I had grown to know in these intimate times ended up carrying me way beyond the accident, even beyond the emergency room and the hospital stay. His presence carried me past recovery and even into the completion of my healing. In fact, it's what carries me today.

I cannot emphasize enough how important it is to develop this intimate REALationship with Jesus before you hit a critical point in your life. Already had some of those moments? It's OK. Dive in now. After all, that's why you bought this book, isn't it?

Trust. It's all about trust when it comes to our relationship with God. Typically, I don't think we trust those we don't know. Often times it takes a while before we totally and completely trust someone, especially with our life. It felt so good when I realized those two nurses went to our church. It gave me a sense of peace knowing there was some kind of common connection that we shared. It allowed me to trust them as they worked on me.

It's the same way with God. So many people in today's society think He is a mean God. They accuse Him of all the bad things that happen in our lives. Not me though, because I already knew Him at this point. I knew Him well enough to know He is a good God who loves me. I could totally trust Him with every detail, including my life. I could trust Him with what appeared to be my lifeless body in His hand. He is the God of resurrection life. He raises us up. It helps to know Him well enough to understand these things. I am not talking about a casual "Sunday only" Christian. I am talking about an "I have been with Jesus and it shows" Christian.

The devil loses again

I saw and experienced the miracle working power of God throughout this whole accident. It would take an entire book to describe every detail of every miraculous thing God did throughout this accident. He healed my broken leg before I even knew it was broken, and there were x-rays to prove it. He even totally removed scar tissue that had developed from the breathing tube. That scar tissue had reduced my voice to a whisper months after the accident. They told me it would be that way forever. In an instant though, my miracle working

God heard our prayers and I coughed up the entire scar tissue, totally healed. Sorry, I don't have a picture for that!

One of the greatest things that came out of this accident was the Gospel of Jesus Christ going around the world. Through the testimony videos made by the 700 Club (CBN.com) and Kenneth Copeland Ministries (KCM.org) thousands upon thousands of people have seen for themselves what God has done. Complete with a re-enactment, testimonies from the actual doctors and nurses, and information from eyewitnesses, these videos have been around the world in several languages. (Watch these videos at: PastorKevin.com.)

The devil miscalculated when he thought he would be able to use this for his benefit. Those two videos have carried the good news of Jesus Christ to more people than I could reach in a lifetime. And the message is still being told. You just read about it and saw the pictures. I feel confident you will tell at least one or two more people about it. God is still getting glory for His miraculous power. Poor devil, he is such a loser, and yet he tries so hard. Poor devil....

CHAPTER 2

What IS This Secret Place?

Let's talk about the Secret Place. The Secret Place is a phrase I became familiar with many years ago. I guess the most common reference to the Secret Place is in Psalm 91:1 where it says, *"He that dwells in the Secret Place of the Most High shall abide under the shadow of the Almighty."* The Secret Place, although not a visible tangible place you can set your GPS to find, is very much a REAL place. It's not about the location as much as it is the reason to enter it and what you do while you're there. The Secret Place is where a person can truly get alone with their Heavenly Father, the One who created them, and the results are life changing!

I will do my best to share with you what the Secret Place is. I will use Scripture as well as my own personal experiences. There are two things I can point to that changed my life drastically. The first is when I took a radical turn and gave my life to the Lord as a senior in high school. The second, is when I went from being a Christian that knew I was going to heaven to becoming a Christian that KNOWS THE ONE who MADE heaven. There is a big difference between knowing about God and actually knowing God.

The Secret Place is that time frame you carve out of your day to learn, live, laugh, love, and linger, with God. It's quality time. It's one-on-One time. It's a breaking time and a building time. It's productive time. It's time in prayer, time in the Bible, time in worship, and time just being quiet. Sometimes it's all these things at once and sometimes it's just one of them. The bottom line is, any time the created is all alone with the Creator, it will have amazing results no matter how it's done.

One of the things I so appreciate about God is that He made all of us different, very different. I am sure your experience of time alone with God could possibly be different from mine. You may be a quiet person when praying and someone else may be a SHOUTER. Some people like a quiet setting while others need worship music playing in the background. We are all different, and that's OK. God made us different for a purpose.

Each one of us reveals a part of God that no one else can express. When we all hook up with God and share Him with the world, they see just how big He really is. All of us together can give the world we live in an accurate picture of God, His Son Jesus, and the Holy Spirit. I've found that the more I get to know the Lord, the more I'm able to demonstrate His uniqueness to the world around me.

This is the wonderful thing about God. He is soooooooo big the universe cannot contain Him, yet He is so personal, He spends time alone with us. No other religion or religious entity can boast about something like this. It is only found in Christianity. So, is the Secret Place to remain a secret? No, but what goes on personally with you and God can be as secret as you desire. I want to tell the world about the Secret Place, about this experience they can have for themselves while here on earth. However, I am certainly not going to tell the world all the secrets, both good and bad about myself, which have surfaced in my time in the Secret Place.

Feeding the hungry

I think the whole idea of spending time with God dropped in me the day I accepted Jesus into my heart. You see, when I gave my life to the Lord as a senior in high school, I was so overwhelmed with this God who loved me that I wanted to know everything I could about Him.

One of the first people who began to disciple me suggested I get a Dake Annotated Reference Bible. I had been looking for a Bible and he said it would be a good one. Well, in case you have never seen a Dake Bible, it is like a reference Bible on steroids. It will gladly fulfill your desire to know all about God. I read and studied it constantly. The more I read, the more my desire for God intensified.

Our church had early morning prayer back then and I began to attend these times of prayer. It wasn't corporate prayer where we all prayed together but it was a time when the sanctuary was opened up and we could go in and have personal prayer time. Little by little God began doing things both to me and through me. Over a period of time, I became more excited about the projects God was giving me than I was about Him.

It's crazy. We get hungry for God, we go after Him, and He fills us and begins to use us to reach others. The more He does, the less we continue to go after Him. Eventually, it turns into nothing but works. Then we have to repent, regroup, and start over again—going after the One who gives us the things to do. Oh, that we would get off this up and down roller coaster relationship with God and become consistent! I want a continuous desire for Him whether He uses me for His projects or not. That's my prayer and I hope it's yours too.

The mystery of Christ in us

I guess the Secret Place is only a secret to those who haven't found out about it yet. For those who do know about it, the only secret is what goes on between you and God. What He reveals to you, and what He works both into and out of your life during this time, is usually personal. You may or may not feel like sharing this information with others. I have journal after journal filled with my experiences from my time with God in the Secret Place. I share some of those entries but some are for my eyes only.

The Bible talks about a secret in Colossians 1:26-27.

"This mystery has been kept in the dark for a long time, but now it's out in the open. God wanted everyone, not just Jews, to know this rich and glorious secret inside and out, regardless of their background, regardless of their religious standing. The mystery in a nutshell is just this: Christ is in you, therefore you can look forward to sharing in God's glory. It's that simple. That is the substance of our Message." (The Message Bible)

This mystery, this "rich and glorious secret," the apostle Paul refers to, is that now Jesus Christ dwells in us. What Jesus Christ has done for us on the cross, and what He did when He rose from the dead, restored the relationship between mankind and God. You and I can experience forgiveness and restoration to our Heavenly Father, through Jesus Christ. This hidden treasure of salvation through Jesus is no longer a secret. It's available for public knowledge. Many people stop with just the salvation of their soul. They don't receive the entire gift by realizing the whole reason Jesus came to earth was to restore this "Father-child" relationship. Many receive Jesus to get their ticket to heaven, and then go on about their own way. That's not what God meant for us. Look, Jesus could not wait to get back to His Father in heaven. There was a relationship there, and of course, it's still there. It's all about a relationship and not just an impressive introduction.

In the beginning, Adam and God must have walked together in the garden. (Gen. 3:8) They had a relationship together, a REALationship. Sin got in the way and became a problem. With Jesus though, this REALationship is restored. We have the opportunity once again to walk together with God. Christ dwells in us and through Him we are reunited with God! Now we should look forward to this intimate REALationship with God. But, as great as that is, this oneness with God is somehow overlooked by many in the busy, fast-paced society we live in. This intimacy with God through a REALationship continues to be a "secret."

The reality that Jesus now dwells inside of us, and what that means concerning our restoration with our Father, explodes when we "dwell in Him." (John 15:4-7) It's through Jesus we can know God personally. That is why Jesus said in John 14:6, *"I am the way, the truth, and the life, and no one comes to the Father except through Me."* It is when we see Him, that we see the Father. (John 14:9) It's all about knowing Jesus and knowing the Father. My question for you is, "Are you dwelling in Jesus?" The Secret Place sets the tone for this to happen.

Allow me to give you an example of identifying the Father by knowing the Son. One time my wife and I were eating at a restaurant for the first time. I noticed that our waitress was looking at me in an inquisitive way. Finally, she said to me, "You MUST be Joshua Kinchen's father!" I had never seen this person in my life and responded, "How do you know I have to be Joshua Kinchen's father when you don't even know me?" She said, "You look exactly like him only in an older body!" Right then I realized this waitress knew the father because she had already met the son. It's the same way with God. We know who He is because we know His Son, Jesus Christ. Jesus is our way to the Father!

If you are already saved, that's awesome. But what about this relationship with the Father? The same way a soul thirsts for the living water that only Jesus can satisfy, our Heavenly Father thirsts for a relationship with you and me. Have you ever been so thirsty you thought you would pass out if you did not find water? I am talking about that kind of thirst. The Father and the Son have already done their part; now it's our turn. So, don't just know you are going to heaven, but step into knowing the One who created heaven. Enjoy this relationship the way God designed it to be, personal and intimate.

A place to dwell or a place to visit?

The Secret Place is actually more of a dwelling place than a place that we visit. God wants us to dwell in Him and not just visit Him. Although we are to dwell in Him, it's typically not something we sit down and do twenty-four hours a day. I have learned there are tremendous benefits if we make time each day for the Lord, time alone with Him.

I can talk to Margie while she is doing dishes—wait, let me rephrase that. Margie can talk to me while I am doing dishes (Come on now, I DO participate in doing dishes at times.), and although I am listening, I cannot say she has my complete and total attention. I know that God is always present and He hears us whenever we talk to Him. The deal is I want to hear from Him! That is why I try to spend time alone with Him, totally focused and uninterrupted time, so I can draw from Him. I attempt to do this every day. Do I always succeed? No. Do I continue to have that as my goal? Absolutely.

Look at it like this: God desires time alone with us. He wants to pour Himself out to you and me on a regular basis. As we hunger and thirst after Him we end up being filled with everything He has for us. The frequency of our time in the Secret Place depends on our desire to be filled with His revelation, His manifested presence, and His power. Here is my own personal "rule of thumb." If I am too busy to spend quality time with God, then I am too busy. And usually, the "busy" is a bunch of things that don't even matter in my life. They are just things.

The "place" of the Secret Place

We talked about the secret of Christ in us and how that's already public knowledge. But, how are we supposed to dwell in Him? Where do we meet with God? The answer... the Secret Place. Now, the Secret Place does not appear on a map. Even Google can't locate it for you because the Secret Place is not a particular place at all. (Even though I do recommend you find a place that is special for you because it does make a difference— more about that in chapter ten.)

Here is how I will describe the "place" part of the Secret Place. I have been married to Margie, my high-school sweetheart, since 1980. As I am writing this book, we have been married thirty years. Even after (aaaalllllll) that time we are still getting to know one another. There are always new things we find out about one another's desires, dreams, and goals.

Margie loves for us to go out on dates when it is just the two of us. I used to think that meant making it all formal and spending a small fortune. I was wrong. Now I am not saying it can't be that way, I am just saying that is not the highlight of the date. What Margie wants is for us to have conversation with one another. That conversation is not to be about work, ministry, or business of any kind, so I found out.

She wants conversation with me and wants it to be about us. (Simple, yet often missed or messed up by me.) God is the same way. In fact, He and Margie think alike. Sometimes we may think the "place" of the Secret Place must be in a church, prayer meeting, or at a retreat center. No, that's not what God is looking for nor is it a requirement. What He wants is you and me. He wants time together so we can talk about us and our relationship together. The Secret Place is anywhere we can meet with God for a personal, undistracted, uninterrupted time. Like I said earlier, simple, yet often missed or messed up by any one of us.

So, how do we get to this Secret Place if it's not a place? The same way I accomplish a successful date. It takes a decision, planning with my wife, and commitment. One thing I've learned is that feelings are not a requirement. If we wait until we "feel" like getting alone with God, when everything is going perfect in our life, it will never happen. Just like a date, the feelings will follow once the decision, the planning, and the commitment to follow through, takes place. That doesn't mean there are no feelings whatsoever. It means we choose to spend time with our spouse regardless of how we feel. In a nutshell, we get to the Secret Place by faith. As you know, faith without action is... dead. (James 2:17) We show our faith in God with our actions to pursue Him.

We need to get into the routine of spending quality time with God in the Secret Place, while not allowing our time in the Secret Place to become routine. Plan to spend time with God but plan to be flexible to His desires once you are there. One night, Margie may want a steak dinner. Another night, it's Chinese food delivered so we don't have to leave the house. The activity we do is flexible, but our time together is something that needs to be consistent. And yes, I am feeling nudged by the Spirit of God that I need to step it up in this area with God and with Margie. Do you see how awesome the Secret Place is?

What does a person DO in the Secret Place?

The next question might be, "What does a person DO in the Secret Place?" And the answer? It depends. It's all about God so we have to see what He wants. We don't want our time with Him to become an impersonal ritual we go through. That's why we need to check with Him. We need to follow His lead instead of our own program. I will share what I do and maybe that will spark something in you.

I don't necessarily have a specific way to enter into the Secret Place. For me, I see it more as a "showing up" for a very important appointment. Listen; let me say this before we go any further. I don't believe God gets mad at us if we don't spend this intimate time with Him. I do however believe He misses us when we don't "show up." I know God is everywhere and around us at all times. I talk to God throughout the day almost every day of my life. However, just as I keep referring to Margie and me in our marriage relationship, I believe there is a difference between casual conversation and time alone with each other.

When I purpose to get alone with God, where I am undistracted and He has my full attention, it's just different. I don't necessarily have to prepare that much before meeting with Him. I just have to plan to do it. I come prepared, but I come as me. Not the "me" I pretend to be. Not the "me" others may think I am. Not the "me" I think God wants to see. I just come as me. I am myself, in the rawest form, ready for God to shape and mold me into His masterpiece.

I usually have my laptop with some great Bible software (www.e-sword.net) and my journal program (Advanced Diary: www.csoftlab.com/Diary.html), ready for studying and taking notes. With my electronic gadgets there is also a great selection of music I have available for worship. Now at this point, please do not picture me sitting by myself with my arms raised in a holy worship-type position. I probably don't have my Bible lifted to God as a token of my appreciation for His presence either—not that I'm against these things—that's just not me.

Instead, I'm probably sitting on our couch or in my office way before the dogs or my family gets up for the day. I may have the latest worship music permeating my mind. I may read something in the Word that morning, or I may just sit there. Sometimes, I might want silence without any music or other distractions, just waiting to hear what God wants to say to me. On mornings when a revelation hits me, I may write down everything I can, as fast as I can. It all depends. It's all about what the Lord is interested in for that day. We learn to follow His lead the best we can. And when in doubt, read the Word. You'll always get direction when you dive into God's Word.

Times and Seasons

People have asked me, "How much time do you spend in this Secret Place with God?" I usually give them the answer I heard John Osteen (Joel Osteen's late father.) give when asked how long he prayed every day. His answer was always, "I won't tell you." Why wouldn't he tell them? If he told them he spends hours and hours in prayer then that person would feel bad because they didn't do the same. If he told them he only spent ten or fifteen minutes in prayer, they may have said, "Well, that's not even enough time to make a difference." How much time anyone else spends with God has nothing to do with what God wants from you or from me.

I remember a season in my life when I woke up anywhere from three to four in the morning so I could go down to our church and be with God. Since I worked there, I would stay in the sanctuary until it was eight o'clock. Do I do this now? Not very often because seasons change. God's purpose in meeting with us at different times, and for different lengths of time, is something He will direct. Don't worry though, He will lead and guide you according to what He is planning for your life. He knows what He's doing and what preparations are necessary.

At that time in my life I had no idea God was equipping me for some upcoming tough times. That in itself made my time in the Secret Place more valuable than ever. God always has a plan. Nothing ever takes Him by surprise. This is why it's so important to spend time in the Secret Place the way God desires. It doesn't matter the way others do it. Suggestions are great, but leave the specific directions to God.

There is life in knowing God

One of the things I absolutely love about the Secret Place is that it's a place for both new believers and seasoned Christians. If a new believer begins to get alone with the Lord, they will become seasoned believers over a period of time. If long-time Christians take the invitation to develop times alone with the Lord, they will find it satisfies, clarifies, and equips their longing to fulfill God's will.

The more I spend time with the Lord the more I realize how much I don't know. I begin to see the need for my total dependence on Him. The verse, *"...without Him I can do nothing"* becomes a revelation (John 15:5). In the Greek, that word "nothing" means "nothing." I don't know how people, even good Christian people, make it through this thing called life without knowing God.

Many people know plenty about God. They can quote Scripture, say all the right things, and go through the designated motions of Christianity. Yet they STILL do not know Him. There is a huge difference between the two. Jesus makes a sobering statement in Matthew 7:23 when He says, *"I never knew you, depart from me..."* That's rough considering He was talking to those who called Him, "Lord." I want to know Him, not just know about Him.

Look, typically, most pastors sell out to the Lord. Yet statistics show that in the United States alone, 1,500 pastors leave the ministry each month and 7,000 churches close their doors each year. Something is wrong. One statistic shows that 80 percent of pastors spend less than fifteen minutes in prayer each day. Seventy percent of them said the only time they spend in the Word of God is to prepare for sermons. That means zero time in the Word to develop their relationship with God.

If you happen to be a pastor or someone in full-time ministry, those statistics ought to pull you into the Secret Place. How can we change the world with a small portion of time being the full diet of our spiritual appetite? It's really no wonder so many churches close their doors when we aren't setting the example for the congregations to follow. I don't want to be a leader or a participant of "spiritual bankruptcy." As individuals, we are the only ones who can determine this. Whether you are a new believer, a seasoned Christian, a pastor, a leader, or part of a congregation, make the Secret Place "your" place to have quality time with God on a regular basis.

Total transformation

Jesus has totally transformed my life as I have committed myself to spend time with Him alone. You know, they always say you become who you hang out with. That is a good thing when you are hanging out with the right people. I can't think of a better one to hang out with than God Himself and His Son, Jesus. The Word says the Holy Spirit will *"guide us into the full truth"* and that He will *"speak what He hears and tell us about things to come"* (John 16:13). I want those things. I want the inside scoop concerning my life.

God always wants to share His goodness and His plans with us. Nevertheless, if we don't give Him the time to do this, I am not sure we'll be open to hear it all. God is an awesome God and it will take all of eternity to get to know Him. Yes, I already have Him in my heart, but I want to continue in the pursuit of knowing Him.

Remember the example I keep using of my relationship with my wife, Margie? Although we have been together for over thirty years we still want to make time for special, uninterrupted, and undistracted time in order to learn more and more about each other. I already "have" Margie but that does not mean I can just leave her on the shelf or just visit her on Sundays. It's the same in our relationship with God. I don't want to have a casual thing going on with Him. I don't want to just stop by and see Him on Sundays. I want to have this quality time with Him where He can say what He desires. I want to be in a place of undivided attention where I can hear Him.

Every minute of our time we spend pursuing Jesus and His will for us is beneficial. His goal for coming to this earth was to restore our relationship with God. Through Jesus, we have this access available to us all the time. God keeps no hours of when we may or may not come to Him. The question each of us has to ask is, "What kind of results do I really want?"

I cannot speak for you, but for me, I am not satisfied yet. Yes, I am complete, but not satisfied. I became complete when I received Jesus into my heart. That was the access. I am not content with just meeting Jesus and leaving it at that. I want to know Him and know His Father. True eternal life is one who knows Jesus and knows His Father. (John 17:3) Do I always "feel" something after I have spent some alone time with God? No, but it's not all about feelings is it? Regardless of a feeling, time with the Lord produces results. It's all about the seed principle. Jesus said the entire Kingdom of God works on this principle.

"The kingdom of God is like a man who scatters seeds on the ground. He sleeps at night and is awake during the day. The seeds sprout and grow, although the man doesn't know how. The ground produces grain by itself. First the green blade appears then the head, then the head full of grain. As soon as the grain is ready, he cuts it with a sickle, because harvest time has come." (Mark 4:26-29 GOD'S WORD Translation)

As we plant the seed of God's Word into our lives, they grow. We may not see a harvest daily, but it's the continual sowing of those seeds that promise a huge harvest when the time is right. Time in the Secret Place nurtures those seeds and welcomes the Holy Spirit to facilitate good growth. Plant the seeds and leave the results up to God. He has a good track record of being extremely faithful, qualified, and skilled at turning seeds into harvests. Sow for your future by planting seeds of God's Word when you spend time with Him. The One who holds a personally designed future for each one of us wants to have fellowship with us. Let's take advantage of this privilege!

CHAPTER 3

It All Started With A Crosswalk

You may be wondering, "What in the world is a crosswalk?" Well, technically, it means to "walk" with a "cross." Go figure, right? Let me explain. Perhaps you have heard of a man named, Arthur Blessitt. (www.blessitt.com) He has carried the cross around the world in every country and every inhabited island group over the last forty years. His cross is twelve foot by six foot and made out of four-inch-by-four-inch wooden posts. He said the cross opened up more doors to share Jesus with people than he could have ever imagined.

Back in 1984 when my family and a friend of ours moved to Nederland, Texas to start a church, I saw Arthur preaching at a Baptist church. I was so impressed with his commitment to the Lord and his passion to take the message of Jesus to the world. When Arthur preached, I knew a seed of his passion landed in my heart and God would somehow use that seed in the future. Little did I know it would happen so soon. I often wondered how Arthur could feel called to do a crazy thing like carry a cross all over the world. Now I know.

Our church in Nederland was a storefront church called, "Church of the Harvest." We created some interesting displays to put in the big, plate glass window showcase to grab people's attention as they passed by. One month we had a big wooden cross in that window. I can't remember our theme, but I am sure it had something to do with Easter.

"Take the cross with you"

We also had an outreach where we ministered to young people who would "cruise the main drag" every weekend. One night, as we were walking out to go to the outreach, the Holy Spirit said, "Take the cross with you." After a thirty second argument about how awkward that would be, I submitted. We must have talked to a hundred kids that night who wanted to know everything from, "Are you Jesus?" to "Why are you doing this?" It was quite the success considering we usually only talked to five or ten people. It went so well, we began to take the cross out every weekend. One thing led to another and before I knew it I was walking from city to city and eventually from state to state.

People from our church, and even pastors, would join me on these crosswalks from time to time. Many people allowed us to pray for them, some gave their lives to the Lord, and newspapers even wrote articles about it. A picture of the cross and me was published in the January 1988, Centennial Issue, of *National Geographic Magazine.* When I saw it was the centerfold of that issue, taking up both pages, it made my head spin. I had been bitten by the Arthur Blessitt "carry your cross to the entire world" bug.

After carrying the cross to such extensive destinations and having incredible results, I began to think about it more and more. That is when my problem began. When we "think" before we "listen" we are like sheep trying to be their own shepherd. It never seems to work out that way, does it? Anyway, I thought to myself, "Man, if so many awesome things are happening on these crosswalks just think what could happen if I was doing it full time." I ran with that thought.

Looking back, I realize that God had definitely spoken to me to start this church in Nederland, but I was the one who had spoken to me about taking the cross across America. That's it! "A-Cross America!" I knew this had to be from the Lord... and yet it came from my own head. Notice I said it came from my head, not my heart; there's a big difference. Before I knew it I had resigned from my church and turned it over to a good friend of mine. I was trading in my pulpit for walking shoes, a backpack, and a new cross. I had never done anything like this before, but hey, I had never been a pastor either. This just had to be God.

You know it's kind of funny, at least it is now. I think everyone but me knew this was not a God thing. It was a Kevin thing. Oh the years of frustration you can avoid IF you will hear what's being said in this book! The value of knowing God intimately is immeasurable. Unfortunately, I didn't have that revelation back then. In my own hype about ME doing something for God, I focused on my own will instead of God's will.

The "thrill" of a self-venture

Margie, my pastor and his wife, even some people in the church, all knew I was about to step into a "self" venture. One person gave Margie a check for five hundred dollars to buy groceries because he didn't know how long I would be gone on my A-Cross America tour. I am cracking up laughing as I type because I just found out about this a few months ago. We are talking about something that happened at least twenty years ago! It is so funny now, but it was no laughing matter back then.

I can't be sure who all knew I was in my own will, and quite frankly, I don't think I want to know. We will just leave it as is. Remember, learn from someone who has "been there and done that." And I really DO have the t-shirt to prove it. Ah yes, the official A-Cross America t-shirts. When in doubt, print it out! That way it really looks official. "Oh Father, forgive me, for I did not know what I was doing."

How could I step away from the church God had told me to pastor and just venture out with nothing but a cross and a backpack? I was the recipient of what I see happening all the time among Christians. I was so excited about doing something for God that I had totally run off with it. I didn't realize I had also run away from the responsibility of a relationship with Him; more concerned about doing than knowing.

You know, as married couples, if you are only excited when you are "doing" something, then there may be a problem in the future. After the doing is over, after the kids are out of the house, after the excitement of it all turns to the work of it all, there will be trouble if the relationship is not a REALationship. There is so much more to a marriage than just the honeymoon. Am I

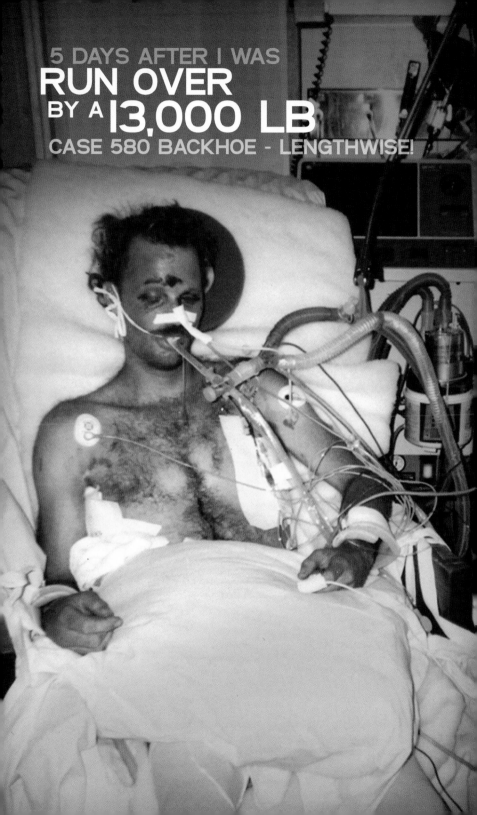

5 DAYS AFTER I WAS
RUN OVER
BY A **13,000 LB**
CASE 580 BACKHOE - LENGTHWISE!

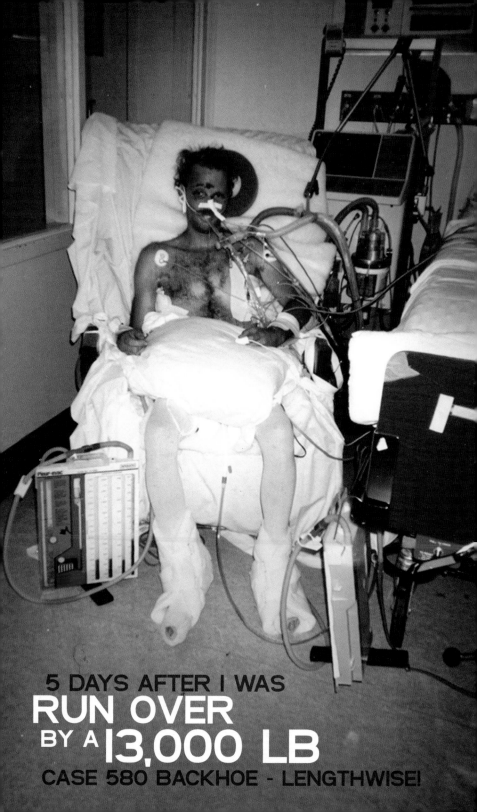

5 DAYS AFTER I WAS **RUN OVER** BY A **13,000 LB** CASE 580 BACKHOE - LENGTHWISE!

13 DAYS AFTER
THE ACCIDENT WHEN
I WALKED OUT OF THE HOSPITAL
TO GO HOME!

After being run over, I had eleven broken ribs, two punctured lungs, a ruptured spleen, a torn liver, a torn ACL in my knee, a gash in my wrist, a possible skull fracture, infections, and what would eventually be determined, a broken leg. Though x-rays revealed a broken leg, God healed it before a cast could be applied. Doctors said the torn ACL would have to be tied back together if I wanted to keep my active lifestyle. God healed that as well and today, I have no residual effects from the accident.

Caption from the January 1988 Centennial Issue of National Geographic: His 90-pound cross had more than a thousand miles on it when preacher Kevin Kinchen rolled into New Orleans to carry the Gospel to Mardi Gras revelers. "I had one without a wheel," he said, "but it got shorter and shorter." The Texas evangelist travels the country on a mission he calls A-Cross America.

CARRYING THE CROSS
IN GHANA, AFRICA
BACK IN 1988

CHRISTMAS 2010

Front Row: Jared/Rachel with Otis, my Mom, Courtney/Grandson #2 - Kooper
Back Row: Me/Grandson #1 - Kallan/Margie, Lauren/Josh/Grandson #3 - Jett

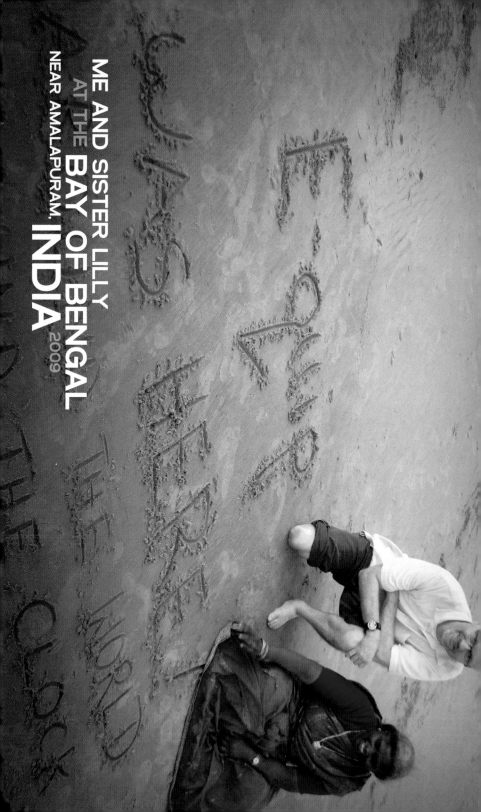

ME AND SISTER LILLY
AT THE **BAY OF BENGAL**
NEAR AMALAPURAM, **INDIA** 2009

right? I had neglected the "knowing" part of my relationship with God and trouble was imminent.

There was also the pressure that came with being a pastor and running a church. The pressure is overwhelming when you are zoned in on self more than Jesus. On the road, carrying the cross, talking to people, and heading to the next destination seemed easier than taking responsibility for everyday things. No wonder it was so easy to convince myself this had to be God!

My goal in carrying the cross to America was pure. I wanted to reach as many people as I possibly could in order to share Jesus with them. Since the day I gave my life to the Lord, I have always had a passion for souls. In fact, the day I got saved way back in 1979 a woman walked up to me and said, *"Son, God has given you a soul-winning ministry."* I had no idea what she was talking about but it must have been a word from the Lord. I still have a passion for the lost. That woman, Mrs. White, is still in our church today as is that prophetic word in my heart.

With that passion and a roaring self-call (God's timing is so vital to the success of anything we do.) I headed to North Carolina. I figured I would start there and work my way to California. Shouldn't be too bad of a journey should it? After all, people need the Lord and I was just the one to tell them. Man, I sure wish I had known the timing thing and the REALationship thing back then.

Oh well, I started out at the beach in New Bern and started walking west on I-70. I had no idea that each footstep was taking me further away from my own calling I had made for myself. God was letting me walk to get "me" out of the way of His will for my life. Each step brought me closer to a valuable principle found in the Bible that changed the course of my life and the pursuit of that course.

The agony of defeat

Every time I carried the cross up until this point, people would pull off the road like crazy. So many people were trying to stop that often times I would hear brakes squealing as if there were about to be an accident. It was like that all of the time, but not THIS time. I began to walk in the hot scorching North Carolina summer sun. I had me, my backpack, some Bibles to give away, and the cross. That's it. I was told on this particular thirty-five mile stretch of highway that there was not a town, store, gas station, or anything for that matter. Too bad my longest day of carrying this heavy cross was only about twenty miles!

I walked and I walked but no one stopped at all. They didn't even wave or honk. Not even a tap on the brake lights. I drank everything I had with me and was beginning to dehydrate. I kept walking and thinking, "Any minute now someone is going to pull over and pick me up." That's how it always happened before. I was so hot and thirsty I thought I was going to pass out. But, I kept walking. In fact, I walked way into the darkness of night. Finally, I could go no more. I was done.

I ended up spending the night on the side of the road with nothing but my backpack, some Bibles, and a cross.

Oh, I forgot to mention the diarrhea I had encountered from dehydration. I was hungry, worn out, frustrated, lonely, and now sick as a dog; and all this on the side of the road. And did I mention, all by myself in a state I had never been in before, on a highway I had never walked, trying to sleep on the ground with bugs? Help!!!

By now, what I thought was a "God-led setup" was quickly turning into a "Kevin- bred mess-up." After the night from hell, I woke up weak and more dehydrated than before. I had no choice but to walk. There was nothing in sight and still not one person was stopping, waving, or even honking. I knew I couldn't walk much longer. It was late in the morning and starting to get extremely hot, again. Finally, when I could not take it any longer, I leaned the cross up against a road sign and put my thumb out to hitchhike to the next town. Guess what? That's right. No one! Not one person even looked interested.

"I took up my cross… and threw it in a bayou!"

Then it dawned on my lightning fast mind, "It's the cross! No one in their right mind is going to pick me up with this big twelve foot cross!" Totally put out with God and feeling like HE had let me down, I shouted my frustrations into the heavens and threw my cross into a bayou, which was running parallel to the highway. I was done with it! "You can have Your cross back, God! I'm done!" I am so glad God has a sense of humor.

With my thumb out once again I was hoping to see some help now. After all, I had got rid of the "burden" the cross created by throwing it in the bayou. I would soon find out it wasn't the cross that created my burden, it was me. The truth is, the cross is a burden-breaker, not a burden-maker. Well, hope turned to despair, as once again, there was not one response. By now my words to the Lord were, "What are You doing to me?" I was stuck. I was all alone and wondering if even God was with me.

I was stuck, but evidently not finished. Even though I was frustrated, upset, and by all indications throwing a spiritual temper tantrum, the Spirit of God was still with me. I was following my own plan while thinking it was God's plan. I was sick, exhausted, and ready to cry. In fact, I did cry. So where is the hope? My heart was right. I wasn't "trying" to be rebellious to God's plan. I was sincere in what I was doing. I wanted to serve God with all my heart and use the passion He had given me for souls as fuel for that service. As long as a person keeps their heart right, there is always hope in God. Truthfully, even when our heart is not right, there is always hope in God. His love for us is relentless.

The "cross-roads" of my turnaround

Suddenly, my miracle showed up in the form of a State of North Carolina Highway Department truck. By now, I was weak, pale, and could barely stand up from the dehydration. As the guys popped out of the truck, one of them stepped up and said, "Man you look bad!" I told him I was extremely sick and needed to get to a hospital or hotel immediately. He offered to take me to a hotel that was up the road several miles. As he put my backpack on the truck, he asked a question that still rings clear in my mind. He said, "Hey, we've been working this highway all morning long. You had a big ol' cross with you earlier—where is it?"

I lost it... not the cross, my emotions! I started crying and told him the whole story. He said, "Look, I'm a Christian too. You can't throw your cross away. Let's go fish it out of the bayou." Wow! The God of hope brought me hope in the form of some highway workers. Little did I know this was the beginning of the greatest turning point in my life other than my salvation. Don't ever think God can't use you on your job. As far as I was concerned, these men were like angels wearing orange safety vests!

After the heroic rescue by these men, I found myself checked into a hotel, weak and famished. There was a large grocery store across the street so I slowly made my way over there. As I walked into the front door of that store, I ran face to face into a bookrack. At about eye level a book stared at me as if it were alive, beckoning me to buy it. The title of the book was, *Discovering God's Will In Your Life* by Lloyd John Ogilvie. (www.drlloydjohnogilvie.com) This was God manifested in "book form" for sure. I needed whatever this book was going to tell me. I got the book and some groceries and hurried back to the hotel.

I poured both the water and the book into my thirsty soul. I read and read and read. I also cried and cried and cried.

Suddenly, it all came to me. I knew where I had missed it. Lloyd Ogilvie said several things that were life-changing.

"The restless search for the will of God is a sure sign that you are out of it!"

"The will of God is not a mysterious set of sealed orders we search for and receive if we happen to hit on the right formula. Rather, the will of God is a relationship with Him in which He discloses His purpose, power, and plan for our lives—and in that order.... The Lord's will for me was to abide, listen, wait—to want Him more than His guidance.... Out of love for me, He withheld temporarily what I wanted in order to give me what I needed."

My entire ministry, desires, dreams, and life were all changed the moment I read those words. I can only pray the same thing is happening in you.

Had I been searching for something I was missing? Well, not really. I think it would be more accurate to say, "Something I was missing was searching for me." You see, I passionately loved God, and still do. But I am also a task oriented person. I would get all excited in my relationship with the Lord, but when He would give me a project to do, I would pull my focus off Him and direct it to the project. I would give 100 percent to the project and totally forget about keeping the relationship intact. Sounds crazy, right? How could I forget God while doing something FOR God?

I have to refer back to my relationship with Margie. She loves and even wants me to do things for her. A simple act of service is one of her love languages. It shows her I love her.

Nevertheless, if I get so caught up in the "doing" but forget her in the process, what good is it? It ends up being, "I will conquer this task to show you I can" instead of, "I really want to do this for you, because you are the love of my life." See the difference?

For months and months I had been asking God, "What do you want me to do?" I never realized His biggest desire was for me to know Him. I realized my priorities were totally out of whack. When we get the revelation of "knowing" versus "doing," our lives will never be the same. That's what happened to me in that hotel room.

To make a long and comical story short, here is a synopsis of the events that took place next. I stayed at the hotel recovering until I ran out of money. Then, I had no choice but to keep walking. I wasn't on the road for more than an hour or so when a lady in a van pulled over with overwhelming excitement about finding me. She said she had been trying to find me for days because she wanted to give me an offering. She wrote me a check for $315.

The check from heaven

Ah, a check straight from heaven! After she drove off I looked and there was a house right beside me. I knocked on the door, told them my story, asked if I could leave the cross with them, and got a ride to the bank and then to the airport. I told that family I would send them some money with instructions on how to ship the cross to me. I sure wish I hadn't lost that phone number. Seriously, I lost it! I hope they aren't still on their porch holding the cross and wondering what happened to me.

The plane ticket was $300 leaving me a few bucks for a meal. I was on my way home. I had learned my lesson and God had rescued me. I was on my way to discovering the Secret Place. God's mercy endures forever!

I went wrong when my focus on the "gift" became greater than my focus on the "Giver." God gave me a gift to share Jesus with the world. Without Him, how good is the gift by itself? That would be like having a new car but yet no fuel to use the car for its intended purpose. It was on this crosswalk, when I was so alone on the highway, that God was able to get through to me. It's amazing how open we are to hearing God's commentary about our life when we are desperate.

I later found out the reason why my wife, my pastors, and others never told me what they thought about my crosswalk. Two reasons: First, I never asked for their opinion and I was too stubborn and set in my own way to listen. Second, I had to find out the hard way. Looking back, I wouldn't trade that experience for the world. God used it to catapult me to the pathway of the Secret Place. Yes, the crosswalk was a miserable mistake but God turned it into a remarkable revelation.

Lessons learned

I actually learned way more than just getting my priorities back to where they should have been all along. I also learned about the importance of Proverbs 24:6 that says, *"In the multitude of counselors there is safety."* Since the crosswalk,

I have done some absolutely crazy ventures with God. Did you notice I said "with" God? The biggest venture was just recently, in 2007, when I stepped away from the security of almost eighteen years on staff at our church. I did this to begin a new ministry in which there was no visible source of income. Sound crazy? It is. This time it was different though. This time I consulted Margie, my pastor, and a good friend of mine. As crazy as it sounded, they all agreed it was the thing to do. Margie was with me this time. And you need to understand, Margie is a planner. She and I are totally opposite. I will jump off a diving board before I even look to see if there is water in the pool. Margie would never do that. She would not only look to see if there was water, but she would test the water for its chlorine level, make sure that certified lifeguards were on duty, have sunscreen in her hand, and then finally jump in the pool. When she agreed with starting this new ministry, I knew it was a God thing instead of a me thing.

I learned something else too. It was appropriate for a crosswalk to be the place where I learned a life-changing principle from God. After all, Jesus did say, *"Take up your cross daily and follow Me" (Luke 9:23).* The cross is a sign of death. In my case, it was the death of self. It was a trading in of my will for "Thy will." It's His will that matters. He knows what makes us tick because He created each one of us. There had to be this dying of self so there could be a resurrection of Jesus inside of me. Have I totally gotten rid of self? No. But, that's why Jesus said to, *"Take up your cross daily..." (Luke 9:23).*

It's a daily thing. Selfish, self-seeking, self-preservation thoughts can pop up any time, sometimes daily. That is why it is so important to surrender to God's plan of time in the Secret Place with Him. Since that hot summer day in North Carolina, I have realized the most important weapon I have to combat the subtly of self. It's an intimate relationship with our Heavenly Father, through His Son, Jesus Christ.

With the help of the Holy Spirit we can stand perfect and complete in all of the will of God for our lives. (Col. 4:12) The more I spend time with Him, the greater the revelation of who He is inside of me. And that's why I humbly say, "I can do all things through Christ who strengthens me" (Phil. 4:13).

Check your priorities. Check your motives. Make sure you are "knowing" more than you are "going." Hopefully, you can learn this lesson at the foot of the cross instead of learning it like I did, underneath the cross. Remember, "The restless search for the will of God is a sure sign that you are out of it." Spend time with the Lord, and His will for your life will follow.

CHAPTER 4

What's A "Hettie?"

Many years ago I listened to a five minute radio program called "Love Talk." The person behind the program was Hettie Lue Brooks from Arkansas. The way she talked about God's love for people was intriguing to say the least. Her voice was unique and memorable. It just "stuck" with me all day long. This "Hettie" and her husband, Don, run a camp in Hot Springs, Arkansas called Brookhill Ranch. (BrookhillRanch.com)

At that time, I had only heard her on the radio. I could tell she really loved Jesus, and it was obvious she really loved people. As I would drive my old Ford pick-up truck, her voice literally came through that radio as if she were in the front seat with me. Although kind of weird, she fascinated me with her love for people. Could someone really love people the way she described? Could someone really put their own desires and disappointments with others aside in order to love people the way Jesus does? It appeared this woman not only thought so, but was living proof of it. It was kind of hard to digest, but I would listen to her broadcast daily. Her "Love Talk" was working both in me and on me, and I didn't even know it.

If you had told me I would someday be talking to that very same "Hettie," I would have told you, "You're crazy!" After all, she lived in Arkansas and I lived in Texas. I had never even been to Arkansas. I am always amazed at how God can put two people together in His own timing and in His own mind-boggling way. That same woman who was coming through my radio would soon be talking to me face to face. Since then, she has imparted things to Margie and me, allowed me to minister together with her, and even gave my two sons an incredible experience at her summer camp.

Yes, this Hettie has been instrumental in my life for sure. It was sometime in the eighties when Hettie came to our church from a request by my pastor. I don't think he knew of my "radio time" with Hettie. Regardless, it was a divine appointment for me. She has been to our church many times over the years, as well as to our Christian school, where she changed the lives of hundreds of young people, including me.

Hettie is the only person I know who can take a group of fifteen to fifty teenagers and have them all day and half the night in one building. And I don't mean locking them in with chains and padlocks. She and her love are so magnetic that she can hold their attention for literally fifteen hours! I saw it with my own eyes! I was there! From eight in the morning until eleven at night, this lady had the kids laughing, crying, acting out skits, praying, repenting, surrendering, forgiving, flowing in the gifts God has for them, and on the edge of their seats. I saw that personally, and I wanted it! I wanted whatever it was she had, and I wanted it bad!

Jesus with skin on

Hettie was the first one I ever heard who used the term "Secret Place." She didn't exactly sit down and preach it to me, she just used that term often. She talks about an intimate up-close relationship with Jesus all the time. She has one of those REALationships with Jesus. It is real and it's her number one priority. When she has her Women's Retreats at their camp, she usually takes their motor home to a lake in Arkansas a week before the retreat. She wants to "hear" what Jesus has planned for each particular retreat. I liked that. It made sense. Once again, I wanted what she had.

You see, Hettie has such an incredible love for the Father, through her relationship with Jesus Christ, that His love for people has rubbed off on her. If you are ever around Hettie for more than two seconds, you will be sure of two things. First, she has a contagious love for Jesus that is visible. Second, you will feel as if you are THE most important person on earth as she talks to you. People can be waiting in line to talk to her and yet she has every bit of her attention on YOU, and nobody but you. I can see Jesus making someone feel the very same way. It is true, you become just like the one you are with the most. With Hettie, that someone is Jesus.

I heard someone say that a little girl was in her room crying because she was afraid. The mother went in, tried to console her, and then reminded her to pray so Jesus would take the fear away. The little girl agreed. After only a few minutes, the mother heard her daughter crying again. Upon arriving at her bedside, she asked her daughter why she was still crying. She responded that she was still afraid. As the mother reminded her once again to pray to Jesus the little girl interrupted and said, "I did pray to Jesus... but I need a Jesus with skin on!"

That is what Hettie showed me. She was living proof that all of us can be a "Jesus with skin on." So far, the only way I have been able to accomplish this is to stick so close to Jesus that there is no room for Kevin to shine through. I know there were kids Hettie dealt with that would have been a test for even the best youth leaders. Funny thing is you would never know it. She treated them all the same. She treated them according to who God had created them to be, not according to who they were at the time. Sounds like Jesus with skin on to me.

She ran out of herself

By now I am sure you have a good picture about one of my heroes. You have to understand, all of this was taking place within a year or two of when I had attempted the crosswalk. God was putting every person, every message, every sermon I could possibly desire in my path for one reason. That reason was to find the key to everything I could ever desire or need, which is exactly what I have been talking about. That key is an intimate and consistent relationship with Jesus.

When I asked Hettie how she learned about the importance of time in the Secret Place, her response was, "desperation." She told me there was a time in her life where she ran out of answers for everything. Actually, she was so desperate that she "ran out of herself." She realized that within herself she could only do so much. If she was going to help people, she had to surrender herself completely to the Lord. Life had to become about God instead of about herself. The apostle Paul said it like this,

"Christ's life showed me how, and enabled me to do it. I identified myself completely with him. Indeed, I have been crucified with Christ. My ego is no longer central. It is no longer important that I appear righteous before you or have your good opinion, and I am no longer driven to impress God. Christ lives in me. The life you see me living is not "mine," but it is lived by faith in the Son of God, who loved me and gave himself for me (Gal. 2:20 MSG).

That's why it's so important for God to occupy the first place position in our lives. Jesus was serious when He said, *"Seek FIRST the Kingdom of God and His righteousness and all these things will be added unto you" (Matt. 6:33).* Hettie was showing and teaching me the value of this, and I was soaking it in and putting it into practice. I did not ever want to re-live another episode like the one I had experienced on that crosswalk. You see, the ministry of Arthur Blessitt had affected me. The ministry of Lloyd Ogilvie had forever changed me. Now Hettie Lue Brooks was influencing me.

What I didn't realize at the time was that all these people had the same thing in common. They had a driving passion for the One who had saved them and called them, Jesus Christ. Now it was happening to me. I was learning to pursue the passion I found in the most influential person ever, the Master, the Messiah, Jesus Christ.

Wrapped up in God

Whenever Hettie would come to our church, or our school, or even when I went to Belize with her and our high school seniors, I was always taking mental notes of how she did things. I was that impressed with the Jesus inside of her. I later implemented everything I gleaned from her when I became the youth pastor for our church. I used those same skills as the camp director for our own summer camp, Victory Camp. I will never forget the one sentence piece of advice she gave me when I became the camp director. She pointed her finger of love right at my heart and said these words, "Don't ever get wrapped up in the *mechanics* of camp; get wrapped up in the *God* of camp!"

Those words are still deep in my heart. It is so easy to get wrapped up in all of the stuff that comes with a calling, or a job, or with anything for that matter. If we allow that to happen, we will end up like me on that crosswalk. We end up frustrated, discouraged, and ready to quit at any moment—burned out. IF we will get wrapped up in God, He has ways of making things work, even the impossible.

Slowly but surely, I was being given the tools that I would need for life itself. The Secret Place was becoming more of a lifestyle than it was a topic to preach about. Hettie was led by the Spirit of God to constantly impart these life-fulfilling treasures into my heart and those around her. She is in her eighties and still travels worldwide and nationwide, preaching the Gospel in churches, schools, retreats, and anywhere else where they need a "Jesus with skin on."

As a bonus, she taught me about "observation"

Hettie also taught me another valuable principle that goes hand in hand with the Secret Place. She taught me how to be observant. Hettie would call people up to the altar right out of the congregation... DURING the sermon! She began to pray for that person, and we would all watch, as the person would begin to weep and then burst into tears. Those tears would be a result of some kind of healing or restoration going on in that individual. I saw person after person set free as she did this. And yes, I wanted that too.

One day I decided to be bold and ask her how in the world she could do that. Did God tell her to call that person up, and if so, why that particular person? Was it a gift of the Spirit or what? She told me it comes from her being "observant." Referring to an incident that had happened in the previous service she said, "Did you notice that girl when you walked into the lobby?" I said, "No." She replied, "Well, I did because I am observant on purpose. I saw her off by herself and noticed she was upset. As I preached, I couldn't get her off my mind. Finally, I realized I had seen her for a reason. That is when I called her up. I had no idea what I was going to say to her, but God knew. The minute I touched her, God showed me what to say and to pray."

God used Hettie's observant eye to help a person become free that night. God is always looking for those who are willing to work with Him and reach out to others. I pray we all desire to be a laborer in God's Master Plan. He has a place for you and for me. Let's take our position and watch what He does with a yielded vessel.

This "being observant" carries right into the Secret Place. I want to observe everything God does so I can be just like Him. What kid doesn't want to be like his father, right? Once again, I think it's that time with Jesus, that time in the Secret Place, which gives a person a love for people so strong it seeks out the hurting. We observe Him so we can notice the hurting. Sounds like another example of Jesus with skin on. Are you getting this?

I'm starting to get the message

So why does it seem God has to use all these people to get one message to me? Well, either it's an awesome message or I am a slow learner. I choose the former. Listen, God uses people in different ways for various things. It's obvious throughout the Bible that God did not do everything Himself. In fact, after creation, He actually moved through people more than He did by personally visiting them Himself. Pastors, teachers, prophets, friends, family, bosses, and even enemies can all be vehicles that the Holy Spirit will use to speak to us.

Is that God's favorite way? I am not so sure about that. I am glad God speaks through me to others; after all, I am a preacher. I wonder if He would love to speak the majority of what He says directly to the people themselves. Think about it. Do you and I always use a spokesperson to talk to our spouse? Well, why not? It's because we want to have a relationship with them ourselves, and it starts with conversation. Hmmm, I wonder if God feels the same way. Often times, we are so busy in our own things that we make no time to listen to God.

Let me leave you with this last thought. Hettie Lue Brooks, and all these others I mentioned were used by God to shape my life with new principles. These principles are now a part of my life. Keep in mind, I was already in full-time ministry and had been the Senior Pastor of my own church when all this was happening. Then I was full-time staff at Living Stones Church for almost eighteen years. All this spiritual activity and yet I was having trouble with the most important spiritual activity of all, time with God. **PLEASE, HEAR ME WHEN I SAY THIS!** (And yes, the **BOLD TYPE** means I am shouting.) No matter who you are, or how spiritual you may think you are, you are truthfully no more spiritual than those you hang out with the most. Period.

That's why God needs to be in that first place position. There can only be one first place; anything else is second. None of us can give away what we do not possess. We cannot impart what we are lacking. I know I have Jesus in my life, but I want a constant flow of the Holy Spirit working through me at all times. I desire something fresh to impart to people. I don't want a plastic, counterfeit kind of love. I want the real love of our God, who IS love, to flow through me. If He wants to talk to me, He doesn't have to search for me. All He has to do is speak; I will be sitting at His feet.

CHAPTER 5

The Two Most Important Questions You Will Ever Ask

The apostle Paul and his writings have inspired me since I started reading the Bible over thirty years ago. Paul ended up writing about two-thirds of the New Testament. He had the ability to share the things revealed to him from the Lord like no other. Through his troubles and his triumphs, he gives us insight on how to live this thing called the Christian life. One of the greatest tools Paul gives us comes from an experience he had that changed everything.

I am talking about Paul's conversion experience where he met Jesus on the road to Damascus. (His name was Saul before he started going by Paul in Acts 13.) Although the actual conversion took place in Acts chapter 9, I want to use the Scriptures in Acts 22:3-10 (GW). This is when Paul was being arrested but was given the opportunity to share his testimony of what happened. He began to tell the people how he was on his way to persecute more Christians. Suddenly, a bright light shined and then Jesus spoke to him saying, *"Saul! Saul! Why are you persecuting Me?"* Saul answered, *"Who are You, sir?"* The voice responded, *"I'm Jesus from Nazareth, the one you're persecuting."* Saul then asked the second question, *"What do you want me to do, Lord?"*

These two questions, if asked in the same order Saul asked them, have the potential to change a person's life. I say this because they are a big part of what changed my life. My pastor taught me that when we see things in the Bible, written in a particular order, we need to keep them in that same order.

Notice Saul's first question was, "Who are you, sir?" He didn't ask, "What do you want me to do?" until after he found out "who" He was. Oh, catch this!

So many well-meaning Christians, like me during that crosswalk, are more interested in, "What we are supposed to do" than we are about "Who He is." We get it backwards. We are all wrapped up in the works and to-do's of our walk instead of being wrapped up in the One who gave us the works and to-do's. Does this make sense to you? We need to KNOW the Lord first.

Let me just say this right away; there is a huge difference in meeting the Lord and knowing Him. Our God is so BIG that you don't just know all there is to know about Him and then move on. Knowing who God is will take an eternal lifetime to fulfill. When we think we know Him, there is always more. Yes, without even knowing it, Paul was setting an example for all of us.

The results from Paul's two questions

When I look at the results of the apostle Paul's conversion, I am amazed to say the least. The voice of Jesus that he heard on the road to Damascus obviously had a powerful impact on his life. Anytime someone has an encounter with Jesus it will result in a completely changed life. The key to sustaining that change lies in the two questions and the order in which they are asked. When you read about Paul giving his testimony of this same encounter in Acts 26:13-19, we see this very clearly.

After Jesus answers the question Paul had asked of, "Who are you?" He tells him a synopsis of what his new life purpose would be.

"Stand up! I have appeared to you for a reason. I'm appointing you to be a servant and witness of what you have seen and of what I will show you. I will rescue you from the Jewish people and from the non-Jewish people to whom I am sending you. You will open their eyes and turn them from darkness to light and from Satan's control to God's. Then they will receive forgiveness for their sins and a share among God's people who are made holy by believing in me."
(Acts 26:16-18 GW)

Paul gets a vision of the purpose God created him to fulfill. We need to realize it was not a vision that laid out every detail for the rest of his life, all at once. We tend to get impatient when we only get a glimpse of what the Lord created us to accomplish. At least Paul knew the right priorities that would allow him to obtain all the specifics he would need for his life. The greatest thing is that now it would be God's plan and direction for Paul's life instead of his own. The key? Get to know Jesus and His Father because they know the purpose and plan for every step of our life.

Paul's passionate pursuit to know Jesus ended up in such a close fellowship that every step of direction was given as needed. Never ever forget, with the exception of a dictionary, the WHO should always come before the WHAT. For me, this daily pursuit of WHO has called me has produced many accurate and incredible directions of WHAT to do.

I'm going to ask the same two questions, are you?

I don't exactly remember when the Lord revealed the importance of these two questions to me, but I know it was years ago. I also know I had probably read those Scriptures many times. I devoured the Book of Acts when I got into full-time ministry. To me, the Book of Acts showed me an example of how church should be. Over time though, I think we glance over things we have read and don't really take the time to soak in new revelation God has for us.

Quality time is one of the great things about dwelling in the Secret Place. It's this time with the Lord that allows us to slow down and listen for His voice. Scriptures come alive as if it were our first time to read them. Remember, the Word of God is alive all the time. It never sleeps and never rests. The Holy Spirit watches over us and has the ability to make one verse impact us depending on what season of our life we are in.

When I read these two questions for the first time and realized the order, the impact, and the results they produced in Paul's life, I began to apply them to my own life. I have never been the same. Little by little, I was beginning to see that the Secret Place, this intimate time of knowing God, would produce change in my life. The more I stepped into my relationship with the Lord the more I desired to know Him. The more I began to know Him the more He began to show me who I am and what I was to accomplish in my life. With each day, the purpose and plan of God for my life became clearer. The best thing about it was the satisfaction and peace that comes when God directs instead of me.

So many people make a big splash into the world of Christianity when they first give their lives to the Lord. At that point and time, if they are anything like me, they are hungry to find out who this Jesus is that just entered their life. Eventually though, when the newness wears off, people often slip into the mode of knowing about Jesus and they lose their passion for

Him. If this continues for any length of time there can come a harsh reality of having "lost their first love."

It doesn't mean they are a bad person. It just means they have drifted away from the Source of the life that changed them in the first place. I don't want to see this happen to anyone, especially you. If we keep doing what we have always done, we will end up with the same results we are getting now. That's why there has to be a change. And in order to change our life, we first have to change our daily routine. I am writing this book in hopes that something will spark that change.

It could all begin with making Paul's questions a regular part of your daily walk with the Lord. Paul tells the Colossians,

"...we haven't stopped praying for you, asking God to give you wise minds and spirits attuned to his will, and so acquire a thorough understanding of the ways in which God works. We pray that you'll live well for the Master, making him proud of you as you work hard in his orchard. As you learn more and more how God works, you will learn how to do your work" *(Col. 1:9-10 MSG).*

Much like the two questions, Paul reaffirms a particular order with these verses. He first prayed for God to give them wise minds and spirits attuned to His will. He also prayed they would acquire a thorough understanding of the ways in which God works. In other words, He prayed they would know God and know how He works. Then Paul prayed they would learn how to do their work. He wanted them to know the ways of the Father so they could learn how to do what God had called each one of them as individuals to do. To know Him is actually God's first thing for our lives. The rest will come. (Matt. 6:33)

Obsessions and answers

By now, you may think I am a little obsessed with Paul's two questions. Really, it doesn't matter if they were Paul's questions or not. It just makes sense. Once again, I must come back to the example of a marriage. I want Margie to know me. She wants me to know her. We both want it. It shouldn't be a surprise that God wants us to know Him as well.

Though Margie and I have been together since we were freshmen in high school, there are still things we are learning about each other. I just found out the other day, after being married for thirty years, that when I go buy her a coffee in the morning, it does more than just settle her desire for caffeine. It's one of the things I can do for her, something that takes me out of my way, which makes her feel special.

For years, I thought it was just her craving for coffee! No, it's more than that. It shows I care. It shows it in a tangible way. Is our pursuit to know our Heavenly Father worth "going out of our way?" Do we even know the things that show God how much we love Him? I hope so. And if not, now sure seems like a great time to ask. I want Him to know there is nothing "too far out of the way" as long as it makes our relationship stronger.

When we ask God, "Who are You?" and "What do you want me to do?" we need to realize the answer to these questions come as a process. In fact, the answers will most likely be ongoing, especially when it comes to who God is. There will not be one answer and we're done. There will always be more to know about Jesus, about God, and about the Holy Spirit. There will also be a "to do list" He has prepared for us the entire time we are on earth. Remember, we are helping Him reach the world with the Gospel, and that is quite the task.

So, it's always progressive. To this day I still receive revelation of who God is and exactly what He wants me to do. You know, once a baby is born, it stares at its parents with that glazed look in its cute little eyes. That baby knows these two towering humans are their "keepers," better known as their mother and father. But, to say that baby "knows" Mom and Dad completely would be a stretch of the imagination. It takes time for a child to know their parents inside and out.

The parents will probably pray over the child, maybe prophesy to them, and even remind them of all they will become for the Lord. But to think those words are all the instruction the child will ever need is unreasonable. Many years of instruction, teaching, and training are necessary for the child to mature and fulfill those prayers and prophecies. It is the same way with the Lord. The process has begun, but it's certainly not finished.

A pattern for our lives

Whenever someone takes the time to find out who the Lord is and what He wants them to do (remember, in that order) something happens. A "process" begins just like it did for the apostle Paul. That person has now triggered a spiritual law that says, *"Ask and you'll get; Seek and you'll find; Knock and the door will open" (Luke 11:9 MSG)*. The Bible also says, *"And if we know that he hears us—whatever we ask—we know that we have what we asked of him" (1 John 5:15 NIV)*.

Listen, God knows everything. He knows it all, and yet we spend the majority of our prayer time doing all the talking. We ask, ask, ask, yet don't seem to hang around afterwards to "hear" anything. God wants to reveal every aspect of Himself to you and me. He also wants to reveal His will for each one of us. He even wants to give us specific instructions and insight into that plan. However, He won't force feed us. He won't make us ask Him the "who and what" questions. But when we do ask them, and are willing to listen for the answers, look out. Lives are about to change because the process has been initiated.

These two questions I keep bringing up are really no more than a way to get us into a pattern for our lives. A pattern is anything that's made to serve as a guide for something being made. Jesus is our pattern. As we allow Him to be our guide, He makes us into His image. He shows us the correct way to "do" life. He is our example of how to love people, how to forgive others, and how to serve the will of His Father. But, He also gave us a pattern on how to live life spiritually.

While on earth, Jesus spent plenty of time in the Scriptures and with His Father in prayer. He knew the Source of His life and He showed us the way to stay attached to that same Source. Even Paul said, *"Pattern yourselves after me [follow my example], as I imitate and follow Christ (the Messiah)"* *(1 Cor. 11:1 The Amplified Bible).* Paul simply gives us an example with these two questions so we can follow Jesus and become connected with His Father.

A life of "Who are you, Lord?" and "What do you want me to do?" will end up acting out the pattern Jesus set forth for us. Jesus told us all throughout the Gospels that HE and HE alone is the only way to the Father. (John 14:6) He also said that He only did the things which His Father instructed Him to do. (John 14:31) So, there it is again... knowing Who God is, by knowing Jesus, and then carrying out what He desires for our lives. Knowing comes before doing. And even in doing, continue with the knowing. THIS, my friend is true life the way God intended us to live.

Unlock the treasures of God's will

"OK, Pastor Kevin, so when is the right time to start asking these questions?" Well, if I were you, I would close this book right now and get alone with the Lord. Yes, I know, it sounds foolish for an author to tell you to put down the book they wrote. But you have to remember, the whole reason I wrote this book is so you will grow closer to God and find His divine calling and purpose for your life.

NOTHING ELSE MATTERS if you don't continually seek to know Christ more intimately. Everything you do outside of Him is futile. Oh, I am sure you could do a lot of good things with your life but that is no guarantee they are "God" things. And listen, if you only pursue this intimate relationship with God in order to find out what you are called to do, then that will be futile as well. Our motive for seeking the Lord through this intimate relationship is to know Him, not to get something from Him. To truly know Him is my definition of a REALationship.

I believe the Lord wants to unlock the treasures of His will for our lives. But the relationship comes first. Look, the devil hates it when God's children start walking in the perfect will of God for their life. It becomes a major threat to his kingdom. God knows that. That is why He won't reveal all of His will for our lives until He knows that we KNOW Him. He does not want His will accomplished at the expense of US.

God never wants to lose a child of His by putting them in the line of fire from the enemy. That's why He has to be sure we know Him first. It's only as we know who He is inside of us and who we are inside of Him that we can successfully combat the enemy. When we know the Lord intimately and personally, it ends up being the devil that trembles in "our" line of fire. When we are confident in *WHO* our Source is, no weapon that comes against us will succeed. (Isaiah 54:17)

I absolutely love you, Moses!

There are many examples in the Bible of this asking "who" before asking "what" idea which the apostle Paul set when he surrendered his life to Jesus. I already mentioned how the life of Jesus was a living example of this. There are others as well. Look at Moses. Here is a man that didn't even *want* to do what he had been asked to do. He was scared, shy, and erratic at times, which caused nothing but trouble for him and those around him. He even had a problem with public speaking! (Exod. 4:10) That's not good considering he was asked to lead a few million people to the Promised Land.

God had put Moses on the earth with a calling and He would provide everything necessary to fulfill that purpose, just like He has done for you and me. As Moses is dealing with the children of Israel, and all their attitudes and complaining, he has a heart-to-heart with God in a face-to-face conversation. (Exod. 33:11) Moses says, *"Look, I've been told to bring up these people. But, You haven't let me know who is going with me... You say that I know your name and I have found favor and grace in your sight" (Exod. 33:12 Author's paraphrase).*

Then Moses says the KEY to it all,

"Now therefore, I pray You, if I have found favor in Your sight, show me now Your way, that I may know You [progressively become more deeply and intimately acquainted with You, perceiving and recognizing and understanding more strongly and clearly] and that I may find favor in Your sight. And [Lord, do] consider that this nation is Your people" (Exod. 33:13 AMP).

I absolutely love you, Moses! What he was saying is, "Show me who You are!" Sound familiar? Guess what God's reply was to Moses? He said, *"My presence will go with you, and I will give you rest" (Exod. 33:14 AMP).* Then, Moses boldly professes, *"If Your presence is NOT with us, I'm NOT going" (Exod. 33:15).* You've got to love this guy! Can you imagine if we would be this way? If we would tell God, "I want to know You! I want to become more and more deeply and intimately acquainted with You!" To think we would want this so desperately that without it, and without His presence, we wouldn't budge another inch in the "doing" part of our calling. Priceless!

The "who" always comes before the "what"

Look at the life of Samuel, a prophet in the Bible. He was just a small boy living in the Temple with Eli. He heard a voice calling him in the middle of the night. He didn't even know it was the voice of God. He kept going to Eli to ask him what he wanted. Eli tells Samuel, "I didn't call out to you." God calls Samuel again and he still thinks it's Eli. Look what 1 Samuel 3:7 in the Message Bible says about it, *"This all happened before Samuel knew God for himself. It was before the revelation of God had been given to him personally."* Samuel needed God to be revealed to him before he could find out what he was supposed to be doing with his life. He also had to know Him in order to recognize His voice.

We are the same way! It runs throughout the entire Bible. The "who" comes before the "what." The Secret Place, your place, where you get alone with God, is the perfect place for you to establish this pattern as well. Get to know who God is so

He can ultimately show you what to do. We need to know Him in order to show Him to a hurting world.

For sure you know by now that I am a fanatic about this alone time with God. In my thirty plus years of being a Christian, I've found nothing else that satisfies, heals, completes, motivates, encourages, directs, purifies, and multiplies my life and the things in my life, like time in the Secret Place. I grow, I change, I'm challenged, and I find joy in knowing Christ through an intimate and consistent REALationship. And according to God's Word, when I know Jesus, I know the Father. (John 8:19)

And *THAT* is life the way God created it to be. Yes, I believe that anything and everything can be found in the Secret Place. It's just a matter of making the decision to dedicate yourself to knowing Jesus and knowing the Father, in a personal and intimate way. So, what are you waiting for? Did you close this book a while ago like I suggested, so you can put this into practice? I hope so. But if not, maybe now is the time. Close this book, follow Paul's example, and say, "Who are You, Lord, tell me exactly *WHO* You are...."

CHAPTER 6

Every Christian's Greatest Calling

I have already mentioned the words "calling" and "purpose" several times. So, before I tell you about every Christian's greatest calling I need to first explain exactly what a "calling" is. Biblically speaking, a calling is something given to us by God. It is something He had in mind even before we were in our mother's womb. (Jer. 1:5; Eph. 1:4) Knowing this alone ought to make us want to know our calling. Who can satisfy the desire of the creature better than the One who made the creature to fulfill a specific calling? The answer? No one even comes close to knowing what satisfies us like God.

When God called me to preach in 1984 I felt kind of like Moses, and said, "Are You crazy?" (With all due respect of course.) I am the one who was so terrified of people it took Valium to get me on stage in a fifth grade play. I am the one who ended up in the psychiatric ward behind lock and key for depression, spurred on from a fear of people. I am the one who was so fearful of people it put me in the hospital for tests time after time with stomach problems. And YOU want ME to preach? Are You crazy? No, He is not crazy. In fact, He is just confident. He is confident that when surrendered, His creation can fulfill the "calling" He put on their life because HE does it THROUGH them. The last twenty-six years of my life are proof of this.

"Who's calling, please?" It's God

So, is my calling the same as my purpose? Technically speaking, it probably is. There is one thing that we must understand though. A calling gives the idea that "someone else" has something to do with it, whereas, a purpose is usually spoken of in a possessive way. It is usually coupled together with the idea that it's "my purpose." I know I am splitting hairs but hear me out. If I seek out "my" purpose and I do not see it as "His" purpose for me then I end up on crosswalk attempts across the United States. (Which you have already read, was not God's purpose for me.) A "calling" makes a person realize there must be someone else involved. Someone is doing the calling.

My wife and I never asked our kids "What do you want to be when you grow up?" Instead, we would say, "What do you feel God wants you to be when you grow up?" We were training them to know God's calling and purpose for their lives instead of their own. There are good ideas and God ideas. We want God ideas for us and our kids... and now our grand-kids. Good is never good enough when compared to God. We shouldn't settle for anything less than God's calling for our lives.

I believe every Christian has a calling given to them by God Himself. Otherwise, He would have brought them up to heaven the minute they got saved. Why would a loving Father keep His newly adopted child on earth instead of bringing them home to heaven, unless they had a particular role to play on earth? We have to realize God is a Master Planner. He PLANNED for you and me to be here. Even if you are an accident in your parents' eyes, you are a vital part of God's plan.

When Margie became pregnant with our daughter, Courtney, we were not trying to have another child. She was a total surprise to us. For years, I think that bothered her. I believe that now, at the age of twenty-one, she completely understands that God planned her to be here. He planned her with a calling. HE called her to be here and HE has a calling for her to fulfill while she is here. And she is well on her way to pursuing that calling. Yes, if you are reading this sentence, have no doubt whatsoever, *Someone greater than yourself has called YOU.* And that someone is God.

When I say God has a calling on your life, don't think it's some random "luck of the draw" kind of thing. No, God has a specific calling for you that is as unique as the fingerprints on your hand. Even though God called me to preach, and there are thousands of preachers in the world, He made me unique. Other people may be preachers but they don't preach like I do. They also won't reach the people God has for me to reach. Does that make me better or worse than them? No, it just makes me someone who God created and placed here on this earth to fulfill a specific thing for His glory.

No one else can do what God called me to do in the way He called me to do it, except me. That is, me as I am surrendered and obedient to His calling. God shows up in me and in you for a reason. If we neglect His calling He has placed on us, there is a unique part of God the world will never see while here on earth. Our uniqueness and calling allow the world to see Him so they can be drawn to Him. I don't want to be the bottleneck that stops up the whole process, do you? I didn't think so.

Called to fellowship with Jesus

OK, so now you understand what a calling is and you understand you are called. I guess your next question would be, "How do you find that specific calling God has for you?" It's simple, just "hang out" with the One who created you for that specific calling. Listen, around the world the question people ask me the most is, "What is my calling?"

I immediately tell them 1 Corinthians 1:9. It says, *"God, who has called you into fellowship with his Son Jesus Christ our Lord, is faithful" (NIV)*. THAT is our first calling we have on this earth. Our calling is to fellowship with Jesus! Our call is to have that upfront, personal, intimate, in your face, close enough to hear a whisper, relationship with Jesus Christ. Whenever I tell this to people they always reply, "I already know that, but I want to know who I should marry, what college I should go to, what is my career supposed to be, things like that?"

The moment they say this I realize, "They didn't get what I told them." First Corinthians 1:9 says, we are "called" into fellowship with Jesus; that means spending time with Him. When we do this with our heart and in a sincere and consistent way, He will gladly "direct" us in the "specifics" of our calling. Once again, there is a sequential order here that we need to keep in place.

I understand the reason for this. I wouldn't want to pour out important information that can change the world to just anybody. I have to get to know them first. I want them to get to know me. Then, and only then, could I give them such crucial information. I would do it over time so they wouldn't be overwhelmed by its world-changing potential. And of course, I would want to see what they DO with the information I give them before I give them more. Makes sense doesn't it?

Hearing the call

Many believers seem to expect to hear God say something directly to them in some kind of BOOMING angelic voice. They act as if God will send Michael the archangel directly to their house with a notarized scroll of parchment detailing every event for their life. Well, if that happens to you, please call me and let me know. I want to know your secret that initiated such a response. For me, it certainly didn't happen that way.

The majority of the time God gives me direction while I'm just "hanging out" with Him in the Secret Place. I am getting to know Him and possibly not even thinking about receiving something from Him. It's then when I will have something "pop out" from the Word of God. Or, maybe I am listening to some worship music, just me and God alone, by ourselves. I will feel a "tug" or a "nudge" in my spirit about something that I know did not come from me.

You see, it's not always a voice that you will hear. Sheep follow their shepherd. They don't necessarily follow only his voice, although that does happen. Oftentimes, they are simply following him so closely they know when to go left or right because they "see" him. They follow his lead. We need to do the same. We need to be so close to Jesus that He can't even turn left without tripping over us at His feet. Stay close and follow the Leader.

Answering the call

As we answer the call we already know for our life, which is to "fellowship with Jesus," He will reveal the things we don't know in great detail. As we are obedient and surrender to what He reveals, He continues to lead us deeper into His will. Once again, it's a process. It's an orderly process that God has designed for us to know His will without the risk of being overwhelmed by it all. If God were to unfold all the details of your life at once He would have to instill His "raising the dead" policy at the same time.

Why do I say that? It's because God's calling for us while on this earth is not anything WE can accomplish on our own. I can assure you of that. If all we do with our life is what "we" can do, then what would we need God for? Many Christians settle for mediocre because it's easier, it's what they can do comfortably. These same people say Christianity is boring. They say it's no fun and not exciting.

Well, living in the limits of our comfort zones, in what we can do, I would have to agree with them. Nevertheless, when you step out of the realm of what YOU can do and into the realm of what God can do, now you have excitement. It's awesome to watch as the Holy Spirit moves through you to change the world around you. When you see the miraculous and supernatural happening through you, call me and tell me, "It's boring." I can't see that happening.

When people decide that spending time to know God is too hard, they have often stepped into their own will. I have been there many times myself. God didn't do what I thought

He should with my life and He didn't do it soon enough to meet my desires. So, I attempted it on my own. Can you say, "FAILURE?" When you and I read the Word of God, which is the voice of God in print, that we are "called to fellowship with Jesus Christ" there is no room for disobedience. If we choose not to do this, we are on our own.

When we do things on our own it leaves us feeling totally frustrated, discouraged, depressed, and ready to give up. This is usually a sign that we may have left our first love. We need to repent and do what it takes to return as Revelation 2:4-5 says. It's only through this intimate and personal relationship that we will know God enough to "trust" Him completely with our lives. For the most part, we human beings don't usually trust those we don't know. And we cannot get to know someone without spending time with them.

I hope you are getting this. I pray God will reveal the gaps, fears, and failures in your life that He alone can restore. He can do this by you getting to know Him and trusting Him all over again. He's waiting.

Addicted to fellowship

Please understand I am not sharing something with you that I just found in a book somewhere. (Though I have read other books on the Secret Place.) I am not sharing something I recently heard about. I am sharing something with you that shaped my life for the last three decades. The more I get to know Jesus in my time with Him, the more I am amazed at what He is able to do both to me and through me. And when I see what He does both to me and through me it gives me the desire to get to know Him even more.

OK, I admit it; I am totally addicted to my time with the Lord. Is it always exciting when I spend this time with Him? No. Is every time in the Secret Place a time where I hear from Him or get unknown direction? No. BUT... the times this "does happen" make up for any of the times when it doesn't. Kathryn Kuhlman, a mighty woman of God who influenced thousands said, "I would rather spend five minutes in the presence of God than a lifetime without His presence." I totally agree with her.

People may think or say, "Well Pastor Kevin, this is something God has told you to do, but He hasn't told me." Hmmm, sorry, I can't agree with that. The verse in 1 Corinthians 1:9 does not have my name in it. It is written to all of us. We are ALL called to fellowship with Jesus. And seriously, why would any of us NOT want this intimate fellowship as a part of our life? I think the only reason why we would attempt to convince ourselves we don't need this is because we just aren't willing to do it.

We don't always have to "feel" like being obedient. We simply obey. Obedience is a choice; whether it's something we feel or not. We make the choice to obey what we are told and shown to do in the Word of God. I cannot imagine any of us heading out for work or for school in the morning while passing up Jesus Christ if He were sitting at the breakfast table. If He had come in and sat down and wanted to chat with us about our lives, I don't think we would say, "Sorry, gotta go; maybe some other time." No, we wouldn't do that.

This is the greatest calling ever, to know the Father and His Son, Jesus Christ. (John 17:3) It is our first calling as well as our greatest calling. Make the choice to fellowship with Jesus whether there's a feeling attached to it or not. The feelings will catch up eventually.

That's not to say the other things God has called us to are any less of a calling. They are not of less importance, but they tend to have limited impact if they are not a result of our relationship with God. Many works "for" God are misinterpreted to be works "from" God. And in a world where being in tune with God is not always a priority, it could be easy to confuse the two.

A work that "looks" successful with all the bells and whistles doesn't necessarily mean it will be a "lasting" work. I want what I do to be lasting. That can only happen when it's inspired and initiated by the EVER-lasting One. When I stay connected to God, I find that the specifics of what He wants for me always come at just the right time. It's when I have His will at the forefront of my life, instead of my own, that I see results. The funny thing is, I know this and yet if I am not careful, I get all caught up in my own will for my life.

It's also easy to get absorbed in the activities of the calling instead of in the activities Director, which is the Lord. Can you see this in your own life? I know I can in mine. My prayer needs to be like that of Jesus, "Not my will be done, but Thy will be done" (Matt. 26:39). I am convinced our true success in life comes from our true fellowship with Jesus Christ.

Intimacy with God IS your calling

This REALationship, this fellowship, these answers and directions about our calling, and our purpose for being on this earth, can all be satisfied in the Secret Place. It's a choice only we can make. And I must tell you, the devil knows this. He knows the closer we get to God the more of a threat we become to his plan and his so-called kingdom. The enemy and all of hell will do absolutely anything possible to keep us from fulfilling this heaven-inspired calling to know God.

Actually, the devil trembles when someone gets the idea in their heart they can "know" God. That's why he attempts an onslaught of trouble to keep us away from anything that resembles a REALationship with Jesus. Remember though, the only power the devil has is the power we give him when we "choose" to believe his lies over God's truth. And the truth is we are called to fellowship with Jesus and to know the Father. That's why there is no better time than NOW to dive in. Stop waiting for the perfect spiritual moment. They don't exist. Dive in now and see what happens. It's all worth it!

"Will the Secret Place help me find my calling?" Whoa, wait just a minute. The Secret Place, this place of intimacy with God, IS your calling. Everything else is just a "result" of that time with Him. Have you ever noticed how couples who have been married for forty or fifty years (Yes, they still exist.) even seem to look like each other? They finish each others sentences and know what the other one wants even before they speak. Come on, you know what I am talking about. Why does this happen?

It happens because it's impossible to be close to someone for that long and not end up with the same characteristics. The more they hang out the better it gets. It just "happens." Listen up! It's the same way with us and our relationship with God. The more we spend time with Him the more we end up with His characteristics. We end up looking, acting, talking, and doing things just like Him. That's a good thing!

Our kids are the same way. If they hang around us long enough, they develop many of our characteristics and habits. That's why we have to set the right example for them. I want my kids to develop my habit of spending time with the Lord in the Secret Place. The result of God rubbing off on me should be all they need in order to see the value in knowing God. We can change the world by changing how we "do" Christianity. It all starts with answering the call to fellowship with Jesus.

The time is now

Whether you're a brand new Christian or someone who has served God since Moses was around, the time is NOW to dive into a fresh and new intimate relationship with the Lord. Like I said earlier, all it takes is a decision. It takes a choice. We don't need to wait for a flash of light or for a feeling. We don't need a prophetic word or a vision from heaven. All we need to do is to step up to the table and sit and dine with the Master. He has already put out an invitation to us through His Word. Now it's up to us.

He WANTS to have some personal time with each one of us. He WANTS to reveal both Himself and His unique plan for our lives to us. Realize the honor of what I am saying here. The King of all kings, the Lord of all, the Creator of the universe, the Savior of the world, the Most High God Himself, "desires" time with us. He has blocked out time, uninterrupted time, for each one of us. How can we turn that down? How in the world can we turn an invitation like this down? I am diving in. And not just once, but I desire to become a "regular." I challenge you to do the same.

CHAPTER 7

Knowing God vs. Knowing "About" God

Knowing God verses knowing "about" God; now that is a great topic for a debate. Many times believers in Jesus Christ feel as if just being a "believer" is the same as "knowing" the One they believe in. Not so. Let me explain. Just because I give my life to the Lord does not necessarily mean I know Him. What it means is, "I have met Him." It means, "I have received Him." However, actually knowing Him is a completely different thing all together. In the Bible, the Pharisees and the Scribes had plenty of head knowledge about the Messiah. They could quote the law, the prophets, everything. Yet, they missed Jesus, the Messiah, standing right in front of them.

The Bible says knowledge puffs up. (1 Cor. 8:1) That does not mean we should all do our best to become ignorant so we don't have to worry about pride. It means knowledge without the Spirit is nothing but a notch in our belt about how smart we are. I would rather know the Lord through my relationship with Him than just know Him from the books I've read or the degrees I've acquired. A saying we use today is accurate concerning this topic, "It's not what you know, but who you know." Boy is that ever the truth concerning Jesus.

The battle for intimacy

This brings up the question, "If God is so interested in us getting to know Him, why does it seem so hard?" Well, my first thought on that is, "Of course it's hard." After all, our relationship with the Lord, our knowing Him, is the most intimidating weapon we possess against the enemy. The greatest battle a Christian will ever face is the battle for "time" alone with the Lord. The building of our relationship with God is something the enemy MUST defeat if he wants to gain ground for his own kingdom. The devil wants to drive a wedge between God and us because it separates us from our Source.

The devil could actually care less about you or me. All he cares about is getting back at God. He is still upset because God kicked him out of heaven due to his rebellious attitude and actions. (Luke 10:18-19) He will do anything at all to keep you and me from knowing the Source of our faith, hope, and love. The devil knows anyone who becomes what God created them to be has the potential to destroy his own kingdom. So, why are there so many things to overcome when pursuing this intimate REALationship with the Lord? There are many things to overcome because this REALationship is the most valuable thing we will possess while here on earth. It's all about "Who we know."

Knowing God is Biblical

Everyone from Abraham to Jesus fought to prevent a wedge of separation from being driven into his or her relationship with God. Abraham had to push past the deadness of his and Sarah's bodies when promised he would have a child at the age of one hundred. Sarah was in her nineties. I'm sure all these things had the potential to get in the way of Abraham knowing and trusting God completely. (Gen. 21:1-7)

Jesus would be exhausted from a day of miracles and would go off to be alone so He could get refreshed in His Father's presence. Right in the middle of it all, here come the disciples or others. (Mark 1:34-37) He had to find time and even make time to be alone with His Father.

In the book of Acts, Peter and John were constantly in trouble for their relationship with Jesus. It wasn't because they had "met" Him. It wasn't because they knew "about" Him. If that were the case all the Pharisees would have been in trouble too. No, it was because they "knew" Him. In fact, it says,

The members of the council were amazed when they saw the boldness of Peter and John, for they could see that they were ordinary men with no special training in the Scriptures. They also recognized them as men who had been with Jesus (Acts 4:13 New Living Translation).

It was visible they had been with Jesus. I want people to look at me and "see" that I have "been with Jesus" too.

Knowing God even though you cannot see Him

How can we get to know Jesus, get to know this God, this Holy Spirit, if we can't even "see" them? I have heard people say it's hard to talk to God because we can't see Him. That's kind of funny, seeing that we live in a society where approximately three out of every four people on earth have a cell phone. They talk all day long to someone they absolutely cannot see. It doesn't seem to be a problem for them, right? "Yeah, Kevin, but that's different because the other person talks back." So does Jesus. So does His Father. And so does the Holy Spirit.

In the Bible Jesus says, *"...the sheep follow him because they know his voice. They will never [on any account] follow a stranger, but will run away from him because they do not know the voice of strangers or recognize their call" (John 10:4-5 AMP).* Well, in order for a sheep to "know" the voice of their shepherd they must have heard him before. Actually, they know the shepherd's voice because they hear it so often.

I think we need to change our outlook on talking to God, otherwise known as prayer. Prayer is not about us doing all the talking. I think God wants to talk to us much more than we allow Him to. The problem is we run out of our prayer closet so fast and never even give God a chance to respond. Remember, it's supposed to be a relationship where both parties talk and both parties listen. It's a relationship where we get to know our Shepherd; a REALationship.

The Word of God helps us with this REALationship. God gave us His Word so we could have something tangible to identify Him. That's why the Word of God plays such a vital part in our relationship with Him. John says it like this, *"In the beginning was the Word, and the Word was with God, and the Word was God" (John 1:1 GW).* Then he says, *"And the Word was made flesh, and dwelt among us, (John 1:14 GW).*

We have to understand the Bible is God's voice in print. The Word of God is ALIVE! Yes, men wrote it, but God was the One giving them the words to write. (2 Tim. 3:16) We have computer programs today that allow you to speak as the program types out what you are saying. Our voice becomes the printed words on a page.

Well, God had the patent on that idea long before any software company came up with it. He has been speaking and directing His words as they show up in print for years. Not only through the Bible, but hopefully He is speaking through the words on pages in books like the one you are holding in your hand right now. Dive into the Word of God as you never have before and allow God's voice in print to reveal exactly "who" He is and what that means for you.

There is only one thing you need

One of the strongest portions of Scripture in the entire Bible is in Matthew chapter seven. Jesus says,

Not everyone who calls out to Me, "Lord! Lord!" will enter the Kingdom of Heaven. Only those who actually do the will of My Father in heaven will enter. On judgment day many will say to Me, "Lord! Lord! We prophesied in Your name and cast out demons in Your name and performed many miracles in Your name." But I will reply, "I never knew you. Get away from Me, you who break God's laws" (Matt. 7:21-23 NLT).

Did you "catch" what Jesus was saying here? I caught that He is not as interested in what we "do" for Him as much as He is about us "knowing" Him. It would be devastating to finally meet Jesus face to face and in the midst of my excitement hear

Him say, *"I never knew you. Get away from Me..."* Ouch! Imagine doing and doing and doing all the wonderful things we as Christians do but missing the most important thing of all; knowing Him.

In Luke 10:38-42 we find Mary and Martha, who were sisters. Martha welcomed Jesus into their home as He was traveling. As Martha was running around like crazy trying to make sure everything looked and tasted perfect, Mary was in the living room just sitting at Jesus' feet "listening" to Him. She was getting to know Him. Martha was after the task but Mary was after the relationship.

When Martha complained about Mary's lack of help, Jesus replied, *"Martha, Martha! You worry and fuss about a lot of things. There's only one thing you need. Mary has made the right choice, and that one thing will not be taken away from her" (vv. 41-42).* Another, "Ouch!" I want to be like Mary. I want to be all about that "one thing" especially when that "one thing" is the "right thing." Lloyd Ogilvie, in his "Preacher's Commentary" says,

It seems to me that the story really deals with our goals in life. What has our attention most of the time? Martha is focused on her own goal. She is so busy being gracious and polite and a good hostess that she has no time to be with the Lord. We may say that all we have—time, life, money—is the Lord's, but does He have our attention? We may be too busy doing good works.

He goes on to say,

You and I can lose sight of who we are and "whose" we are very easily. The good things in life—family, job, community service, even good works—can begin to choke out God's life in us. As we make God and His presence in our lives our primary focus, we find HE is the key to everything.

I think Lloyd Ogilvie said it all. My prayer is, "Lord, help us to be like Mary so we can be all about You."

The benefit of knowing God

If someone comes to church on some Sunday where I am preaching they will be able to meet me. If they came back that Sunday night for a second service, they would not only have met me but they would also know some things "about" me. The more that person comes to services where I am preaching, the more they eventually learn about me. Nevertheless, it would be an overstatement if that person went around telling people they "know" me. Why? When we only have a one-sided conversation, it's impossible to ever "know" someone.

It takes dialog to know someone. It takes interaction and plenty of time to get to know them personally. It doesn't happen overnight. Many Christians have a one-sided relationship with Christ and yet still say they know Him. As my example illustrates, that would be a stretch of the truth. Now my wife knows me. My pastor knows me. My good friends Jim and Kathy know me. In fact, they all know me inside and out. Of course, that's because we have all made time to get to know one another. It didn't just happen. Time and dialog are huge factors in this building process.

Relationships don't happen because we bump into one another at church every Sunday. They take time, effort, dedication, and commitment. It's the same with Jesus. It takes time, effort, dedication, and commitment to really know Him. Are we willing to do what it takes to know Him? If so, the benefits far outweigh the battle it takes to develop this relationship.

Seriously, how can I know God?

I will talk more in detail about specifics concerning "how" to know God in some of the following chapters. But for now, I want to at least plant a few seeds in you. We can take some practical steps every day that will move us from knowing "about" God to actually knowing Him.

First, we need to make the choice we are going to do this. Make the decision to be committed to this REALationship with God. Be consistent with it. Consistency is something that seems to be disappearing more and more in today's society, but consistency is a key factor in knowing God. God is consistent with His ways even though His techniques are as different as the grains of sand in the sea.

Being consistent in your relationship with the Lord shows faithfulness. Remember what I said earlier, "Get into the routine of spending quality time with God but don't let your time with Him become routine." Be open to what God wants each time you are with Him. As you are faithful in cultivating this REALationship your life will see changes that will amaze even long-time believers.

You should *ALWAYS* have something to take notes with when you have these times with God. Anything the Lord shows you or speaks to you is certainly worth writing down. In fact, we need to be prepared to write down what the Lord speaks to us throughout our entire day. (Record your voice on your cell phone if you have to.) It's so important to document what the Holy Spirit shows you. Remember, you are building a relationship here. The more you know Him, the more you recognize His voice. And the more you recognize His voice, the more you are going to hear from Him. After all, He's been talking all along because friends talk. Get ready for it.

Finally, remember you are not spending time with God to earn something or to get a handout. You are spending time with God to KNOW Him. Don't ever let this time turn "mechanical." Keep it what it really is, the building of the greatest relationship you will ever have in your life; a REALationship.

Knowledge based or Knowing based

Do you remember that Dake Reference Bible I told you about? It is full of thousands and thousands of notes written by Finnis Dake. Well, back then I would dive into those notes of his like crazy. One note would lead to another and it would literally consume me for hours at a time. I was also reading tons of Christian books and magazines during that time in my life. I will never forget when the Lord dealt with me and said, *"When are you going to take a break from learning ABOUT Me and get into the Scriptures so you can actually KNOW Me?"*

I learned a valuable lesson that day. Books aren't bad. That should be obvious since you are holding one of mine in your hands. Everything needs balance though. Studying about God is not the same as getting to know Him in the Scriptures. The Scriptures are alive and able to change us like no other manuscript ever written. Before I knew this, when I first started preaching, I would study my Bible like crazy to get a sermon for Sunday. When Sunday was over, I would start all over again. This went on for months.

Then, one day the Lord spoke to me again. He said, *"Stop reading your Bible to GET a sermon. Study it to KNOW Me. Then, I will give you more sermons than you can preach in a lifetime."* That was over twenty years ago and I still live by that principle today. Keep an eye out for little warning signs that you are slipping into a knowledge-based relationship with the Lord instead of one formed from a relationship with Him.

I pray you are being motivated to dive into a REALationship with the Lord like never before. I pray you're moved from knowing about Him to actually knowing Him. I say that because motivation is always a better teacher than frustration. That is how I ended up tapping into the Secret Place. God turned my frustration into the motivation to KNOW Him. My life changed forever when my focus became knowing Jesus.

All that frustration took place while I was in full-time ministry. If you are in full-time ministry, take this advice. Finish reading this book and begin to put these principles into action. Then, after a week or so, read it again. Once you have done that, go and buy Bob Sorge's book, *Secrets of the Secret Place (www.oasishouse.net)*, and read it over and over again for at least a year. Why all this? It's because those of us in full-time ministry can be the worst when it comes to spending quality time with God. These books motivate you to "know God" through spending time with Him.

Remember, we cannot effectively lead others when we aren't even following the same principles we preach. We cannot give away what we do not possess ourselves. It's not good enough for me to only have knowledge "about" Jesus so I can tell a congregation "about" Him. No, I want to possess Jesus, to know Him, to have a fresh REALationship with Him. Then I will be able to impart Jesus to the congregation instead of just feed them a band-aid dose of knowledge.

Undivided Focused Time

The Secret Place is an avenue the Lord gives us to know Him. It's a time where you and God can meet alone. Margie and I can certainly talk throughout the day and we do. We have been working side by side for many years. We can talk while driving, while working, while watching TV, even while getting ready to start our day. Even with all of that conversation, we still need undivided focused time together to experience a thriving relationship. We need time alone, time alone for intimacy, time where there are no distractions.

For years and years, we would take two weeks for vacation each year. One week would be with our kids. The other week would be without our kids. Why? We needed time alone. I remember when our kids were little and one of them asked, "How come we don't get to go with you and mommy on the second vacation?" I responded, "Do you like mommy and daddy being married and staying together?" They said, "Yes." To which I replied, "Well let us go then!" Come on now, you know it's true. We all need quality time to build strong relationships!

It is the same way in our relationship with God. He is always with us and He is always available to talk no matter what we are doing. I am telling you the truth when I tell you something HAPPENS when we dedicate a segment of our day specifically to our Creator. Let the Secret Place be your second week of vacation. The only change you need to make from my example is you need to make the Secret Place your second week of vacation, DAILY, or at least as often as you can. I have found that DAILY is the best for me.

So, am I talking about a weekend retreat or something of that nature when I talk about the Secret Place? No, that's not what I mean, although weekend retreats are great. I am talking about a completely new mindset. I am talking about rearranging whatever is necessary to accomplish some time alone with God. For me, it meant a new way of living. I was not a morning person back then but I am now. My goal for every day of my life is to "report to God first." I know that sounds somewhat militant but that's how serious this is.

You are going to see this clearly in the next chapter. This is not a "thing" we do and at a certain level of maturity, we stop. We will be getting to know God from now throughout all eternity. He is so big there is no way to contain Him. Why do we sometimes think we already "have it" when it comes to knowing God? I want to grow in my relationship with the Lord... always.

If we are not growing then we cannot produce fruit. We MUST stay attached to the Vine to produce fruit. Well, Jesus is the Vine and His Father is the vineyard keeper. (John 15:1-7) I don't know of any fruit-producing vine that is connected one week but disconnected the next. No, for me, I want to stay connected. From what I have found out over the last twenty or thirty years, intimacy with God, time alone with Him, on a daily or regular basis is the best way to accomplish this.

Visible fruit

As we stay connected to Jesus, the fruit is visible. I mentioned earlier about Peter and John, and how people could see, "they had been with Jesus." How could they know this? It's always visible when a person has been with Jesus. Always. Jesus is a master at imparting Himself to others. You cannot be in a REALationship without it being visible. Now, don't get this confused with a person who knows "about" Jesus. That shows too, but usually not in very good ways.

A person who knows about Jesus without actually knowing Him tends to be judgmental, critical, condemning, prideful, arrogant, and overall unpleasant to be around. Do NOT think those are qualities of someone who knows Jesus. What is Jesus like? He is loving, kind, merciful, forgiving, caring, and a sold out optimist. When it comes to us, His children, He is notorious for believing in us when we don't even believe in ourselves. He believes in us to such a degree He even laid His life down for us. He did this while we were still sinners. (Rom. 5:8)

If that is how Jesus is, then as we spend time with Him, we will show those same characteristics as well. The more we get to know Him the more we become like Him. He imparts Himself to those that are with Him. That's why His disciples ended up changing the world. Jesus was visible through them. Though they were common everyday people, people who had all kinds of quirks about them, Jesus was still able to shine through them. He was able to do this because they were always hanging around with Him.

In fact, the disciples were so determined to be in His immediate presence, He had to sneak away at times just to be by Himself. I want to be like the disciples... in the presence of Jesus so I can receive the full impact of what He has for me. What about you? I believe your desire to fellowship with Jesus is growing. In fact, I can see you becoming codependent; in a good way. I see you becoming so dependent on this intimate relationship with God that you can't live without Him!

Knowing the Father comes through the Son, Jesus

The only way this "knowing" God can ever take place is through Jesus. Jesus Himself said He is the ONLY way to the Father. (John 14:6) I have been all over the world and have seen people serve and worship everything from statues they say are "gods" to people who have been dead for a long time. And not one "religion" I know of (Except Christianity.) boasts that you can actually get to KNOW the god you worship. In fact, they require so much out of the person in this cold legalistic way of life, there is actually no life at all; only works. THAT is why Christianity has life. It has life because our God IS alive. Jesus IS alive!

For the most part, I wrote this book for Christians, for believers. However, I know God well enough to know He will slip this book into the hands of those who do not know Him. He will make sure people, who have never received Jesus Christ into their lives, find it and read it. If YOU happen to be one of those people, why don't you ask Jesus into your heart right now? Invite Him into your life.

Way back in 1979, I said a big long prayer like this to invite Jesus into my life. I said, "Jesus, I want you!" That's it! I said it and I meant it with my whole heart. That was and still is the greatest thing I have ever done in my life. You can pray and receive Jesus into your life too. It is without a doubt the greatest decision you will ever make in your life.

Once you've prayed and invited Jesus Christ into your heart, realize that was only the introduction. You have now "met" Jesus. Now comes the relationship part. Get a Bible and read it so you can KNOW Him. Get to know Him for the rest of your life. He will take care of life's details as you come to know Him more and more. Oh, one more thing... Welcome to the family, the family of God!!!

Here is my last thought on this topic. (If you just received Jesus into your heart this is vital information for you.) We need to make sure we surround ourselves with other believers who also desire more than just knowing about God. We must surround ourselves with people who want to KNOW Him. We need to be involved in a good Bible based church where we can hear messages about having a relationship with God. A church that's alive with the Spirit of God.

The Bible tells us "Iron sharpens iron" (Prov. 27:17). When we are with like-minded people, we tend to sharpen each other. As someone shares with me how God is drawing him or her into a closer, more intimate relationship, it motivates me. Likewise, my pursuit in developing an intimate and personal relationship with the Lord will bless others.

As we continue building this REALationship, we will begin to see results we never could have imagined. There is nothing more satisfying than having the King of kings and the Lord of lords share Himself with us personally. As I have already said, it is so worth whatever effort it takes. It's worth it beyond measure!

CHAPTER 8

Psalms 91 - How One Chapter Changed My Life

As you can plainly see by now, God has made huge changes in my life to draw me into this close-up intimate relationship with Him. One of the greatest changes He performed in my life is the reality of truth that we find in Psalms 91. When the backhoe ran over me, I had spent good quality time with the Lord before I ever went to the camp. After the news spread to our church right across the street, my pastor, Al Jandl, heard about it. He was told the accident was serious, life threatening serious.

I was bleeding out of my eyes, ears, nose, mouth, arms, and who knows where else. Pastor Al immediately bolted out the front door of our church to rush to my side. The Holy Spirit stopped him though. God dealt with him to go back into the church and pray. He ran back into the church and said, *"God! What can I do for Kevin?"* According to Pastor Al, immediately the Lord spoke to him out of Psalms 91:14-16, which says:

Because he loves me, says the LORD, I will rescue him; I will protect him, for he acknowledges my name. He will call upon me, and I will answer him; I will be with him in trouble, I will deliver him and honor him. With long life will I satisfy him and show him my salvation (Ps. 91:14-16 NIV).

When Pastor Al told me what the Lord had spoken to him on that day it hit me like a ton of bricks. Through these verses, God was telling me personally, *"Kevin, because you love Me, I will rescue you; I will protect you for you acknowledge My Name. You will call upon Me and I will answer you; I will be with you in trouble, I will deliver you and honor you. With long life I will satisfy you and show you My salvation."* What had I done to deserve this? Nothing, absolutely nothing. All I had done was get to know the One who has known me forever. Knowing God brought on a completely new meaning after this.

As I told you earlier, the benefits of actually "knowing" God far outweigh the battles you fight in order to do so. Yes, it can be difficult to find time to get alone with God. Yes, it can become discouraging when you feel like it is doing no good at all. Yes, it makes you change your entire schedule and perhaps your way of life. And yes, it is difficult to do consistently. BUT... YES, it saved my life! YES, it gave me a hotline to God! YES, it made it to where I am going to LIVE looooooooooong on the earth! This is what you have to look at. Time with God always pays off, always!

God's promise of protection

Some might say, "If Psalms 91 is all about protection in the Secret Place, how come you were run over by the backhoe? That doesn't sound like protection to me." Well, in answer to this question, let me just tell it like it is. First off, the reason I was run over by the backhoe is because I was stupid enough to stand next to it. Plus, I was in between the front and rear wheels, while trying to start it. THAT, my friend, is a stupid thing to do! So, technically, that's why I was run over.

OK, spiritually speaking, think about that word "protection." It means something is evidently attacking or coming against the protected. If not, why would there need to be protection in the first place. Where there is no enemy there is no need for protection. The Bible says, *"No weapon formed against us will prosper"* (Isa. 54:17). It does NOT SAY that weapons won't come; it just says they won't prosper, they won't succeed.

There is an enemy out there and he's against all believers. His name is satan. (No capital letter for satan on purpose.) He is always in the attack mode hoping for some kind of success to bring us down. The key for us is to know he cannot prosper with these attacks because of WHO we KNOW.

I have zero effects in my body from that accident. It's as if the accident never happened, except for one thing, the testimony of what God did to "rescue" me. That testimony has gone around the world in several languages bringing hope to thousands. Yes, God protected me all right and I am so thankful for it.

I believe when we get to heaven we will find out God protected us many times before tragedies took place. In the Bible, God was constantly giving His people insight and information to protect them. Specifically I can think of Joseph and Mary, the apostle Paul, Peter and John, and the woman caught in adultery. I am sure there are many more examples as well.

Have you ever wondered why for no reason at all, you took a different way home? Have you experienced a delay for a flight because they wanted to change planes? Has there ever been the unction to stay away from certain people? All of these situations could possibly be some of that "protection" that comes from knowing our Heavenly Father.

The protection of Psalms 91 continues

God has saved my life several times since the accident. After a hard fall down some stairs in 2003, I suffered from severe back pain. For five and a half years, many doctors, surgeons, neurologists, pain specialists, therapists, and chiropractors did all they could to help me. I had many extensive procedures done beyond description. I felt like the woman with the issue of blood in Mark 5:26. I had *"suffered a great deal under the care of many doctors and had spent all I had, yet instead of getting better I grew worse."*

In an attempt to relieve the pain, doctors performed a surgical procedure on me. Not only did it fail to relieve the pain but it also gave me a deadly staph infection inside my spinal column. Not good. They said once again, *"This could possibly take your life."* If I did live, the doctors said it's possible I could end up paralyzed from the infection. Not good either.

By a series of what I will call "miracles," I obviously came through. Not only that, but they finally found and fixed the problem in my lower back with a fusion. I have some valuable steel in my back now but I am pain free. In fact, I have been pain free from the day they operated on me and am still pain free as I am typing this book.

Psalms 91 is more than some "name it and claim it" formula. It's a life-changer. It's a life-changer that shows when we are connected to God, He is not only faithful to the relationship, but He is indeed a lifesaver. And the death threats continued... you won't believe the next one. Keep reading, who knows what chapter it will show up in....

We cannot deny that the more we know God the better off we are. Too often we want to justify why or how this doesn't apply to us. We think we are the exception to the rule. Well, we can think it all we want but that certainly doesn't make it true. The truth is, Psalms 91:1 says, *"He who dwells in the Secret Place of the Most High shall remain stable and fixed under the shadow of the Almighty [Whose power no foe can withstand]."* IF we do "our" part, we can rest assured God will do "His" part. Our part is to dwell in the Secret Place. He will take care of the rest.

It's a dwelling place not a twice-a-year vacation place

You can read Psalms 91 in any translation and you get the same idea. You get the idea that as we get to know God and stay connected to Him, He will take care of us and protect us like any good father would. Notice verse one says, *"He who dwells in the Secret Place..."* What it does NOT say is he that visits the Secret Place or he that vacations in the Secret Place. It gives us more of a solid, stable, and permanent kind of word by saying *"He who dwells..."* This is why I believe it should be a regular place of retreat for us. Please remember I am not talking about having to be in some sanctuary or at an altar. I am talking about a place where we can slip off to in order to get alone with the Lord.

Oftentimes, when I get alone with God, I smack a pair of headphones in my ears, open up the Word of God, and just like "that" I am in my own sanctuary. But the key to it all is realizing it's a dwelling place. It's a place where for those moments we aren't in a hurry and we aren't buried with thoughts about our to-do list. We are focused on God. Nothing else matters. It's our alone time with God.

I know if there are mothers with young children reading this it can seem impossible to do what I'm talking about. Alone time is not something you get to experience very often. Get creative. God will help you with this. It may only be a few minutes in between naps, or when you are in the bathroom with the door closed. Whatever it takes, it will certainly be worth it. God is the One who can "make a way" when there seems to be no way. (Isa. 43:19)

The shadow

As I kept reading verse one, I also noticed where it said if we are dwelling in the Secret Place we would, *"remain stable and fixed under the shadow of the Almighty."* Think about that for a minute. When we "dwell" we are "under the shadow" of the Almighty. In order to be "under the shadow" I would think that means to be close to the person. After all, it's kind of hard to separate a shadow from its owner, right? I have never had anyone call me and tell me, "Hey Kevin, your shadow is over at our house again." That would be impossible. My shadow can only be where I am.

This confirms the whole idea of knowing God verses knowing about God. If I am UNDER God's shadow then I am close to Him. I am not in a distant place just gathering knowledge about Him. I have to be with Him in order to be under that shadow. It makes sense doesn't it? What's my point? It's all about the relationship. It's about intimacy and being close. It's all about making this daily feeding of our spirit a regular and permanent part of our lives. God desires us so much. I want to make sure I am available to satisfy His desire. In doing this, I am confident He will satisfy the desires of my heart.

It's a "father" thing

To me, Psalms 91 is all about a "fatherly" relationship from the father's perspective. I know we see all the benefits God promised to us, and I love those. Nevertheless, being a father who loves my three children, two daughters-in-law, and three grandsons, I see it from a different perspective. The love of a father is beyond comprehension for someone who has never been one. The overwhelming desires to love, protect, and provide for our children is incredible. And when denied, is heartbreaking.

Recently, Margie and I were out of state preaching. Our twenty-one-year-old daughter, Courtney, who lives at home so she can go to nursing school, was staying by herself. Early one morning I received a call from the alarm company telling us our back door had been shattered and the alarm was going off. I told them my daughter was home alone and to please call the police. We tried hysterically to contact Courtney on her phone but could not.

A few minutes later, the alarm company called back. They said someone at the house who thought there was a burglar in the house with them, called the police. As you can imagine, my mind kicked into overdrive that someone had broken in and was holding my daughter as a hostage or even worse. The most painful thing for me was the fact that I was in another state, hundreds and hundreds of miles away. I soooooooooooo wanted to be there to protect her!

I was heartbroken that "distance" denied me my parental rights to be a "father" for my daughter. I cannot accurately describe the emotions, frustration, and helplessness that overcame me at that moment. God feels that same way about us. Too often our "distance" from God denies Him of His parental rights to be a "father" to us. Oh, how that must break His heart! We distance ourselves from His presence and shadow by being too busy with "things." And most of the time, they are things that don't really matter. In the whole scheme of life, they don't really matter at all.

The joy that overtook me when I finally heard my daughter's voice was a wave of smiles and tears at the same time. She was OK! We found out a big decorative plate that had been hanging on the wall had fallen and shattered. It is what set the alarm off. When Courtney heard the crash and the alarm, it jolted her out of bed thinking someone was in the house. Locking the bedroom door and dialing the police were her immediate actions. The police came in record time (And so did my son who I am sure was breaking every traffic law ever written... but I'm thankful for his own "fatherly instincts.") and checked the house out just in case. My daughter said she has never been so scared in her life.

Though she did not create this incident, it still illustrates my point. When we are distant from our Heavenly Father, spiritually speaking, it's easy for fear to come when we are put in troublesome situations. And from God's viewpoint, distance often denies Him His parental right to protect us from that fear and whatever caused it.

I don't ever want to let distance in my relationship with God cause Him to feel the way I did that morning. I don't want my distance from Him to be what denies Him of His parental right to love me, protect me, and provide for me. That's why my daily goal is to stay close and connected to the One who loves me more than anything, my Heavenly Father, God Himself.

We get so much for only one act of obedience

Psalms 91 gives us one thing that is our responsibility, to dwell and abide in Him. The majority of the next fifteen verses spell out all the benefits we get for this one act of obedience. It reaffirms this in verse nine where God speaks and says, *"Because you have made the Lord your refuge, and the Most High your dwelling place..."* Then He goes on with more of the benefits.

With what we have already covered in this book, and now in Psalms 91, I hope a revelation of the Secret Place is coming on you. The God of the universe desires time with us. He wants to have conversation with us. He wants to be our shield, our protector, our refuge, our fortress. He wants to be our everything. That's why His name is, "I AM." It's because, He IS. (Exod. 3:14)

No matter what we ever face in our lives, God is our answer to it all. Jesus Christ paid the price for us to become one with the Father, just like He is one with the Father. I don't want the price Jesus paid to go to waste. The price He paid is worth way more than just our salvation. I am not discounting our salvation but realize it is only part of the whole picture. Why not take advantage of everything that God so desperately wants us to have. HE wants a REALationship with you and with me. He wants that relationship when we get to heaven but He also wants it now, while we are still on earth.

At one point in my walk with the Lord, I felt impressed to read nothing but Psalms 91. I read it again and again for weeks. The more I read it the more it came alive on the inside of me. Too often, we rush our time reading God's Word. When we just read the Bible with no relationship in mind eventually the print becomes just words on paper. If we make an effort to keep the relationship as our motive, it will be life changing.

When our hearts are open to what God has to say to us we find that His Word will transform us to become like Jesus. I am no one special. By that, I mean God didn't give me some kind of a supernatural ability to spend time with Him. I am like everyone else. I struggle at times. It's not always easy, but it is always worth it. Reading Psalms 91 gave me the realization that I simply cannot afford to live life any other way. Time with God is a must for me. I pray it's becoming a must for you too.

Becoming a lifetime partner

As a preacher, I can be reading along in my Bible and certain verses seem to "pop out." I know I will end up preaching on that particular verse eventually. When I got into Psalms 91, it was different though. Oh, I knew I would preach on "abiding" and "dwelling" in God, but it was more than that. I knew God was giving me another opportunity to see how anything and everything is available in this Secret Place.

I knew my Heavenly Father was transforming me to become a lifetime partner with Him.

This is not a relationship based on works. It is not about how good or how bad I am. It is all about the love and the desire God has for me. He is passionate to see that I fulfill everything He has planned for me. I know I've said this already, but it bears repeating. If I know anything at all, I know our quality time with our Heavenly Father and His Son, Jesus, is by far THE most important thing ever!

You know, I don't want you to get the wrong idea here. I am not some super-duper, naturally diligent, perfectly spiritual person that easily floats around all day in and out of the manifested presence of God. Just ask my family, they will tell you. I do feel sold out to God though. I do feel I desire this time with Him much more than anything. Even with Margie, I love her like no other, but she knows she is second when in line with God. She wants it that way.

Margie and I both know that without a daily "hand-in-hand" walk with the Lord I am not always a pleasant person. She can tell when I have been with Jesus and when I haven't. It's THAT important. Husbands and wives, listen up! Jesus, and especially time spent with Jesus, is the absolute best thing for your marriage. When you have been in fellowship with Jesus it's so much easier to be the husband or wife you need to be. Without that fellowship, we are pretty much on our own. So far, I haven't been impressed with what I can do on my own. Frankly, no one else is impressed either.

You are a lighthouse

Are you convinced yet? Are you finding yourself wanting to get alone with God? Do you sense a new hunger for time with Him? Can you hear Him knocking on the door? Do you have time to let Him in? I pray you are "catching" what I have desired to impart to you with this book. I feel it's what the Lord desires as well. He wants to impart Himself to you in supernatural ways that will become contagious.

People will "catch" what you experience in your time alone with God. Oh, you may have to throw in a few words now and then to explain what they are seeing in you. But for the most part, all you are doing is "letting your Light shine." You found the key that turned the switch on. You are no longer some little LED light that can barely be seen. You are a LIGHTHOUSE that people will see for miles. You are a lighthouse that helps people make it through the storms of life. Oh, just go ahead and admit it. You are becoming a "Jesus with skin on." Awesome!

CHAPTER 9

Does God REALLY Wake Up At 5:00 AM?

I ask—ask the God of our Master, Jesus Christ, the God of glory—to make you intelligent and discerning in knowing him personally, your eyes focused and clear, so that you can see exactly what it is he is calling you to do, grasp the immensity of this glorious way of life he has for Christians, oh, the utter extravagance of his work in us who trust him—endless energy, boundless strength! (Eph. 1:17-19 MSG)

I think this is one of the most powerful portions of Scripture in the Bible. Just look at it. God wants us intelligent and discerning in, "knowing Him personally." Wow! He wants our eyes focused and clear (spiritual as well as natural) so we can see "exactly" what He is "calling" us to do. Wow again! Do you remember the two questions I already mentioned? Who are You, Lord? What do You want me to do? Well, here is that basic principle again only this time it's from God's perspective. He wants us to know Him personally and He wants us to see exactly what our specific callings are.

Then, He even goes so far as to say He wants us to grasp the immensity of this glorious way of life He has planned for us. This makes me want to know Him and His plans like crazy. I feel like any time spent working on "my" little plans are a total waste of time. I know I have wasted lots of time trying to accomplish my own things, or even attempting to do His things, but in my own way. This does not work at all. Especially when compared to what He has planned for us. Stay open minded as you read this chapter. I want to share some specifics about spending time in the Secret Place in order to "know Him personally" and to "see exactly what He is calling you to do." I want you to see a principle in the Word that makes sense from His view but can be difficult to see from ours.

There is something special about the "early" morning

OK, obviously I don't really think God wakes up at five o'clock in the morning. As far as I know, He keeps no hours and doesn't need to sleep. Nevertheless, He does believe in some kind of organized time because He makes the sun rise and set at specific times every day. We happen to live in a society that definitely runs based on this thing called time. People typically start their day at a certain time. They go to work or school at specific hours, they eat at certain times, they sleep at specified times, and the list goes on.

So, back in the 1980s there was a lot of teaching about having a prayer time early in the morning. The chosen time was usually 5:00 a.m. Many churches would open up their sanctuaries at 5:00 a.m. so people could come and pray. Connected with a teaching on the Lord's Prayer, it was actually a great idea that helped many people. I happen to be one of them. But why 5:00 a.m.? Well, I am not sure about the specific hour of 5:00 a.m. but I do know why it was "early morning." Here's why. *"In the morning, long before sunrise, Jesus went to a place where he could be alone to pray." (Mark 1:35 GW)*

Way back in the '80s I was NOT a morning person at all. I had noticed there were a number of times where Jesus would leave the crowds to get alone with His Father. He would find a place where it was quiet, where He could be undistracted. Well, when I came across verses like Mark 1:35, I saw that Jesus got up so early in the morning that it says, *"...long before sunrise."* Jesus is our example. He is our pattern to follow. There had to be a reason for Him to get up that early. He had just performed many miracles and cast out many demons the night before, yet He got up early to get alone with His Father. From what He was showing me, I knew a radical change was heading my way.

Now, in the year 2010, I am a definite believer of getting up early. There, I said it. You knew it was coming. Why do I think it's necessary to get up early? For one thing, Jesus did. Next, Matthew 6:33 talks about seeking the Kingdom of God "first." To me, first means first. There can only be one first. I want Jesus to be in that first place position when it comes to my life and calling. I want Him to be first in my giving, my dedication, my motives, in everything, including my day. If Jesus is REALLY as important to me as I have just described, then I believe seeking Him "first" before I do anything else, is essential.

Giving God your best instead of your leftovers

I already said I was not a morning person back then. The Lord must have put a desire in me to change though. (I hope He will do the same thing in you as you keep reading.) Here was my thinking in all this. If I truly want God to be first place in my life, then I need Him to be first on a daily basis too. We are told to pray, *"Give us this day our daily bread" (Luke 11:3)* and to *"take up our cross daily" (Luke 9:23)* in the Word of God.

It made perfect sense to me that I needed to START every day with the Lord before I went to work.

I decided to meet with God before I became involved in each day's activities. I wanted to "report to God" first. I already mentioned that "glorious way of life" He has for us as described in Ephesians 1:18. I wanted to tap into THAT kind of life before I started each day. I still desire this glorious way of life. I am now a morning person. In fact, early morning before sunrise is without a doubt my favorite part of any day.

Does this mean I don't talk to God at any other time during the day or night? Of course not. Nevertheless, I have found in those early hours, once I have taken my shower to wake up, that I am fresh. I am not in a hurry, I am undistracted, and I am able to focus on the things of God better than any other time of day. In fact, if I oversleep and everything has already begun for the day, it's difficult for me to settle down and get quiet before the Lord. Once the phone is ringing, people are out of bed, and I am checking my schedule to see what I have to do for the day, the day is on. My "work" mode has already kicked in by then.

I want to give God my best. I want to give Him my "first fruits" so to speak. If I attempt time in the Secret Place at night, I feel like I am giving Him my leftovers. Worn to a frazzle from working, I just crawl before Him and offer up what is left after a stressful day. Does He get mad at me for that? No, but He deserves better than that. He deserves my absolute best.

The Bible says in Proverbs 8:17, *"I love those who love me, and those who seek me early and diligently shall find me"* *(AMP).* It also says in Psalms 63:1, which is a Psalm of David when he was in the wilderness of Judah, *"O God, You are my God. At dawn I search for You. My soul thirsts for You. My body longs for You in a dry, parched land where there is no water"* *(GW)*.

If you look up that word "early" in Proverbs 8:17 it means: *to dawn, that is, (figuratively) be (up) early at any task (with the implication of earnestness); by extension to search for (with painstaking), enquire early, rise (seek) betimes, seek (diligently) early, in the morning (Reference from Strong's Concordance).* I am not trying to be legalistic here and "make" you or anyone else seek the Lord first thing each day. What I am doing is telling you that in "my" life, I have seen HUGE results from doing so. I cannot tell you all the miraculous things the Lord has done each day since this practice has become a part of my life.

I don't think these verses are in the Bible just to take up space. They are in there for us to see and to implement as a way of life. For this to happen there has to be a different mindset. Instead of trying to "work a time for God into our schedule," we must determine to "work our schedule around our time with Him." THAT is a life-changing statement. It all has to do with, *"Seeking Him first..." (Matt. 6:33).* And first always means first. I know this next statement is strong so "gulp" before you read it. "First means first, and either He is or He is not in that first place position in our lives." Enough said.

Jesus is our example

Earlier we read Mark 1:35 where it says, *"In the morning, long before sunrise, Jesus went to a place where he could be alone to pray."* In order to see exactly what happened here we need to know what happened before and after this verse. Before this verse, Jesus had been healing people and casting demons out of people. It even says the whole town gathered outside His door. Revival was on! This went on into the evening and probably into the night. Then, Jesus gets up before sunrise to get alone in His Secret Place. The disciples came looking for Him and when they found Him, they told Him the crowds of people were looking for Him and desired to see Him. THIS is when it gets good. In verse 38 Jesus tells the disciples, *"Let's go somewhere else, to the small towns that are nearby. I have to spread the Good News in them also. This is why I have come"* (GW).

Hear me on this. After huge revival services where people want you back for more, it would be so easy to go that direction. I know myself, as a preacher, I would rather go where the people love me and desire me, than go into a new territory where they may not even listen. I am just being honest. Jesus KNEW His Father had given Him other instructions. He was not going to go the direction of the flesh, the direction of the least resistance.

Where do you think Jesus got the strength and motivation to choose the less popular option? Did His Father remind Him of "why" He had sent Him? How did He even know the specifics of His calling? I think Jesus received all these things during His time alone with His Father. In this example, He woke up early in the morning, and spent time alone with His Father, in His Secret Place. If it was an important thing for Jesus then I want it to be important for me too.

Life-changing and Life-saving results

If staying focused on my calling is the only benefit from spending time with the Lord early in the morning, it would be totally worth the effort. That in itself would motivate me to set my alarm clock. And look, that doesn't mean you have to get up at 5:00 a.m. or it doesn't count. Remember, I am not talking about a law here. I am talking about a principle, a way of life.

Since the Lord taught me about the Secret Place, and then added this principle of giving Him my "first place" time each day, I have seen drastic changes in my life. So much that it would take another book just to tell you everything. I have received revelation from the Word of God, ideas on how to save thousands of dollars for our church, correction, peace beyond comprehension, direction, doors of favor opened, even life-saving wisdom for others. It did not happen because I am so great. It has happened because such a Great One desires to spend time with me, and He has given me the grace to do it.

One of those "life-saving" experiences from this early morning time with God involved my oldest son, Jared. One morning as I was coming out of our sanctuary, after being in there for quite sometime, I heard the Lord say, *"You aren't through. Go back in and pray."* Even though I had no idea what I could have missed, I obeyed. I prayed in the spirit for about thirty or forty-five minutes. At one point during that time, I prayed for Jared. Eventually, I felt a release that assured me about everything I prayed for. I knew something spiritual had taken place.

The "second" I walked out, I received a frantic phone call from Jared. He was crying out, "Dad, I've been in a bad wreck!"

He had been in a horrible accident and was in an ambulance on the way to a Trauma Hospital. I picked up Margie and sped to the hospital emergency room. He was messed up bad. His leg had been broken in half about five inches below the hip. He was in excruciating pain.

A police officer, who had been right behind Jared when he wrecked, was in the hallway. He told me Jared had slammed into the back end of a parked utility truck that was working on a guardrail. The truck was not in sight to Jared due to a big truck that was in front of him. As Jared was looking to change lanes and enter the freeway that big truck dodged the parked truck and Jared hit it doing forty-five miles per hour. The police officer told me Jared never even had the chance to hit his brakes. He told me my son should not have lived due to the extent of the wreck.

Jared's head shattered the windshield though he wasn't cut. (I had always told him he had a hard head.) He also needed surgery to fix his broken leg. The officer said it was a good thing I was not at the scene. He said, "I have never heard anyone screaming with pain like your son as we straightened his leg to get him out of the car."

I asked the police officer when the actual wreck had happened. I was shocked when he told me the time. It was the exact time when I had been praying in the spirit after God had directed me to stay and pray. I know those prayers saved Jared's life. God had indeed given me instructions on what to do "that day" just as He had instructed Jesus in Mark 1:35. I am so glad I was seeking the Lord early that day. Oh, and so is Jared!

Becoming a morning person

"All right, I get it. But, how do I become a morning person?" Don't you love how I speak "for" you? I sound like a wife don't I? *JUST KIDDING!* Anyway, first off, you need to ask the Lord to give you the desire to be a morning person so you can spend time with Him. If you don't even desire to ask for this, then pray He will give you the "desire" to ask. Now that you've asked, believe you have received, and then put forth actions to show you really do believe you have received. (James 2:17)

Here, let me help by offering some actions I had to do. First, we need to change the way we think. Since this is a priority, we need to create our daily schedule "around" this time with God as much as possible. If we wait for the time to open up it will never happen. Never! Second, we may have to cut out some of that late night television. Remember, what are our priorities? I would rather hear from the Lord than from any late night talk show host or a movie.

Next, set your alarm. Sometimes I set more than one. I do not want to miss my appointment with God. Finally, pray. Every night when you go to bed, after you have set your alarm(s), pray and ask God to wake you up so you can meet with Him. Every time I do this, I wake up a minute or two before the alarm goes off, regardless of how early the alarm was set for. I think it's God's way of saying, *"I can't wait to see you in a little while!"* Take this seriously. It's time to get serious about "getting serious about the things of God."

Please remember, God is not mad at you if you don't do this. He does not get mad when you oversleep or just cannot do it. This is not a bondage thing but it is something He has honored and blessed in my life. Sometimes, the day I oversleep is when God will pour out some kind of blessing that blows my socks off. I think He does that just to remind me it's not all about how good I am. It's about how good HE is. But that doesn't mean I am going to sleep in every day to see if I get an even better blessing. That would be ridiculous.

In fact, it's on those days where I received the incredible blessings that I can't wait to get up early the next morning. Why? I can't wait to spend time with the One who is so good to me. I want to give Him what He desires. What does He desire? He desires ME. He desires YOU. Let's not allow our "distance" to keep God from being able to satisfy His parental desire to show us, His kids, the affection of His heart.

It all started to make sense

As all these things start falling into place you will realize the same thing I did. I noticed as I kept my motive to "know Him" and as I honored Him by giving Him that first place slot in my life, everything began to make sense. The Bible says, *God's ways are not our ways and His thoughts are not our thoughts* (Isa. 55:9). When I read this, the Lord spoke to me and said, *"I want you to start thinking the way I think."* I told Him that was impossible. That verse plainly says His thoughts are NOT our thoughts. That's when He replied, *"Show Me where it says it has to STAY that way!"*

After a few quick thoughts and a second look at the verse I replied, "Well, er, um, it doesn't say it has to remain like that." He then said, *"Exactly. I have given you the mind of Christ, start thinking like Me."* I am not smart enough to come up with things like this on my own. Statements from God begin to flow to us and through us as we dive into this intimate and personal REALationship. God allows things to make sense as no one else can. It's called revelation knowledge or, His wisdom revealed.

Yes, meeting with God early in my day involved massive changes in my life. It has been difficult at times. I had to learn how to get over the condemnation I would bring on myself when I failed. Days and even weeks can go by without ever feeling like God is anywhere around.

Here is the good news. We can press on until we break through. We can do it because we make a choice and we will not be moved according to our feelings or emotions. God is always faithful and He gives us the promise that if we seek Him with our whole heart, we will find Him. (1 Chron. 28:9) As we hunger and thirst for His righteousness, we WILL be filled. (Matt. 5:6) Any amounts of tests, trials, or troubles we have to push through in order to develop this intimate REALationship with God are worth it.

Tap into a new realm

We tap into another realm when we start honoring God for Who He is. Something takes place when we put "our" plans aside and start finding and following His plans. Unfortunately, many Christians have lost respect for who God really is. I know He is my friend, but He is also my Lord. As I honor Him with my time, money, and entire life, He in turn honors me for showing that honor. I want to reverence God. What does that mean? It means to show Him respect.

God is not an invisible nothing we talk to. He is GOD. I have been in my Secret Place time before and after downing a cinnamon roll earlier, a "burp" finds its way to the surface. Us Kinchens' are very accomplished "burpers." But if I do that when I am in the Secret Place, all alone with God, I say out loud, "Excuse me." Why? It's out of respect. I treat God as if He were there, because He is. If I were standing in front of a king, or anyone else, I would say, "Excuse me." So, why not say it to God. He is the King of kings isn't He? Of course He is. He is worthy of our honor. We honor and respect the Lord our God when we start our day with the One who "makes" the days. Is it law? No. Is it good advice? Absolutely.

Let me close this chapter by reminding you just how much God desires to spend quality time with you. His thoughts toward you are more in number than the grains of sand in the sea. (Ps. 139:17-18) Why not allow Him to lavish those thoughts on you? Let Him have enough of your time for Him to love you the way He desires. I promise you will not be disappointed. I pray you will tap into all the great things that come with seeking Him first.

Father, I am asking You to give everyone who is reading this book the desire to seek You first. Give them the desire to start their day with You, to report to You first. Help them to be able to wrap their mind around this concept. Give them a good taste of how good You are. I also pray you will give them the ability to push past any obstacle that may attempt to stop them. Give them grace to stick with it until Your Son returns to get us. Show them You are alive and desire to meet with them. Do Your stuff, God. Just do Your stuff!

CHAPTER 10

What Am I Supposed To Do In The Secret Place?

OK, so you're convinced the Secret Place is something you are going to apply to your life. (I say that in faith.) You desire quality time with God so you can truly KNOW Him and His ways. You might be wondering, "What in the world do I do when I get alone with God in the Secret Place?" Great question! I will share with you what works for me. Keep in mind that I get up early and have developed what works for me over many years. You and God will come up with a plan that works for you.

After I get up, because I set my alarm the night before, I grab my juice and something to eat and head to my office or to our living room. I may even go outside. I just want to be somewhere alone. I have my laptop or my iPad with me for my Bible study and notes. I also have an idea of what I will read in the Word. I have found it's extremely beneficial to have some kind of a Bible reading schedule or plan to go by. The old "close your eyes and point" method will not paint the whole picture the Bible presents to us.

God gave me a systematic way that takes a person through the whole Bible in two years. I love having two years instead of one so I can take it slow without rushing through it. If you read thirty-two verses from the Old Testament and eleven verses from the New Testament each day, you will read the entire Bible in two years. I call it the, "32/11 Bible In Two Years Reading Program." Now that's an original title isn't it? If you don't want to count the verses every day then go to my website (www.PastorKevin.com) and download a file that has them all listed out. And yes, it's free.

If a particular verse jumps out at me then I jump into that verse and find out everything I can about it. I do this using other translations, commentaries, and a listening ear. I also usually have some praise and worship music on to help me stay focused. I write down everything the Holy Spirit shows me about that particular verse. You will be amazed at what God shows you when you give attention to the Word of God like this.

When you are spending this time with God, make sure you settle yourself, try to avoid distractions, and give God the freedom to direct you. If you feel no direction, you can't go wrong with reading the Word. Read it and express to the Lord how grateful and thankful you are that He came into your life. OK, there you are. At this point, we have shown up and we are ready for life-changing encounters with God.

Do what God wants to do

Once I am settled and ready for my "appointment" with the Lord, I try my best to stay open to what He desires. I usually start by reading the next portion of Scripture in whatever reading schedule I am using. From there, only God knows. But, that's OK. I may read a verse that stirs me up to pray for someone. I may not get anything out of what I read and therefore, I sit there, waiting on the Holy Spirit to "enlighten" me. I will read that portion again and usually see a difference. If not, when time allows, I will keep reading until I do get something out of it.

Sometimes I find myself sitting and saying absolutely nothing. Since I am the one who knows nothing, I need to be quiet and listen to Him that knows everything. I have to remind myself, "Let God have a chance to say something."

Worship is also a big part of my time with the Lord. By worship, I am not necessarily talking about me singing and dancing all around the place. Some do that and it's awesome. I am a bit more reserved. I will just sit and soak up the words in the worship music I am listening to. I am more apt to "speak" my praise to God than I am to "sing" it. I don't think He minds at all. In fact, as I am typing this, I have some awesome worship music playing right beside me. I sense the presence of the Holy Spirit and I love it. Somehow, I think God loves it too.

Remember what I said earlier, the Secret Place is something we want as a part of our daily routine, but we don't want what we do in the Secret Place to become routine. If a person starts out with an "I will try this out to see if it works" attitude they have already defeated themselves. We are not getting alone with God to "get" something and if we don't "get" it, we quit. The only thing we are expecting is to get to know Him more.

Let me give you a word of caution here. Don't become discouraged if it takes you a while to settle down enough to become completely focused on the Lord. Our flesh is used to being in control. We can become fidgety and uncomfortable when being taught to submit. It might take a month to actually get alone with God and feel like you actually tapped into something. That whole month you may have spent most of your time beating the flesh, which is the human nature side of us, into submission. Stick with it. The day will come when you can't wait to get alone with God so you can be in His presence.

How long and how often?

Time; it's something we never seem to have enough of but yet there is no way to manufacture more. So what is the correct amount of time to spend in the Secret Place? "As much time as we can" is my answer. Look, we are all different. God knows that. All He wants is our best. He just wants each one of us to give Him our best.

There have been seasons where I have spent three hours or more dwelling in the Secret Place on a daily basis. This has gone on for months at a time. I would get up at three or four in the morning and go down to our church to get alone. My life is radically changed during times like these, but there is a grace to do this. Without His grace, I would have never been able to do something like that.

There have also been times where I could only give God a half hour or even less. It was in those times, when I was giving it my best effort, that the Holy Spirit changed my life in radical ways as well. The bottom line is to give God our best and to do it with a willing and open heart. Always think of it like this, we are building a REALationship with God, not going to a job. Though God might be someone's employer, like in my situation, He is first and foremost our Father. Build a REALationship with Him.

For me, time alone with the Lord is a daily thing. That is my goal. I don't always fulfill that goal, but it is still my goal. Without a vision, people perish; they run wildly. (Prov. 29:18) I always keep the vision of daily time with God before me. I need the guidance, the insight, the revelations, the strength, and everything else God has for us on a daily basis. Time with Him once a month, here and there, is not enough for me. I know some say, "Well, I am different, I don't need quality time with God every day." Are you sure?

Unless you have experienced this "daily time" for yourself, you don't really know if you need it or not. For years, I never thought I "needed" glasses. Then, I got some. I saw things I had been missing for years. I didn't realize how bad my sight was until my eyes became focused and could see clearly. Now, unless God does a miracle, my glasses are on my face every day; because I like seeing the WHOLE PICTURE. I think you get the "spiritual" meaning of that illustration. Don't assume you don't need something if you've not yet experienced "that" something.

I have several reasons for a daily time with the Lord. First, Jesus said to His disciples "Pray like this... Give us this day our DAILY bread" (Luke 11:3). He is not talking about "natural" bread here, because He had already told them as they sought Him, and His Kingdom, they would not have to worry about what to eat or drink. (Matt. 6:25, 31-33) Our spirit man needs this daily spiritual bread. Jesus IS that "Bread of Life." (John 6:33, 35, 48, 51).

The children of Israel experienced the "natural" side of daily bread when they were in the desert for many years. Though it was actual bread, better known as manna, it was a "type and shadow" for the spiritual bread, we receive from Jesus. They had specific instructions for gathering manna each day. They had to gather the exact amount they needed for each day. If they tried to gather more than needed, so they could take the next day off from manna gathering, the extra manna would spoil and rot. The only exception to this was the day before the Sabbath, which was the Lord's Day.

I know this is Old Testament but the principle of it still holds true today. We shouldn't try to live today on yesterday's revelation. Each day our life is different, so we need to tap into what God has in store for THAT day. We need daily manna, daily bread from heaven. What if I am wrong about this? Hmmm, how can getting to know God more and more each day be wrong? I don't think it's possible. Let's just give Him our best. He will set the pace and the duration for each one of us.

Baggage policies for the Secret Place

My number one goal while IN the Secret Place is to give God full control over my life as I get to know Him more and more. Jesus has already paid the expensive price for us to experience true life. Life that is free from guilt, condemnation, fear, worry, sickness, poverty, and a whole list of other things. He has set the example for our lives by being in perfect unity with His Father. We are to experience this same unity with God. The reason we don't always enjoy this ultimate life is because we usually have too much extra baggage we try to carry around with us.

Just like the airlines, there is a price to pay for those extra bags. You pay when they are too heavy as well. Listen, guilt, condemnation, fear, worry, and all those other things should be "prohibited baggage" for you and me. Who wants to pay extra when Jesus has already taken care of all our needs?

It's IN the Secret Place where I find myself with "lost" luggage too. Only this time, it's a good thing. The more I hang out with Jesus the more He reveals I don't really need to carry a particular bag anymore. Before you know it, something I have dealt with or something that's been a lifelong problem is completely gone; LOST! Did I do it? No, I just sat in His presence long enough to where the extra bags just dropped off. That's when I become changed into His image from glory to glory. (2 Cor. 3:18)

That change can spread to others. Nothing we ever do, both with and for the Lord, ever affects just us. There is a trickle down affect on those around us and those we meet. Here is a prime example. I hope that the times I have spent in the Secret Place are going to have an affect on you. I am not writing this book to become something great. I am writing it because of something great that has happened in my life. I write about it and share it with others so they can experience what I have experienced. What starts in one person can make its way to hundreds of people in a short period.

That is how life works. The more we hang out with the Lord, the more He rubs off on us. By rubbing off on us, it erases that "unnecessary baggage" we used to carry. And let me tell you, when someone gets on a plane, people always notice those who seem to travel so light, and those who travel with way too much. People will certainly notice when we travel through life with only a "carry-on" of peace instead of the overweight baggage of fear, worry, anxiety, trouble, bitterness, and other weighty things. Trust me, they notice.

Listen before you speak

It's easy to think like this, "I talk to God throughout my day and I am sure that's good enough." Well, that all depends on who is setting the limits of what is "good enough." Are we saying this according to "our own" assessment of good enough? Or, is it God's assessment? Have we even asked Him, "Hey

God, would You like to have some of my undivided attention?" If we haven't asked, maybe we ought to.

We serve a jealous, passionate, "crazy in love with us" God. I think it's awesome when we talk to God throughout the day; I do that too. What's even MORE awesome is when we can talk to Him throughout the day ABOUT the things that happened in the Secret Place that morning. Woo Hoo! There is nothing like telling the "manna Maker" how good His manna was that day. It sure beats talking to Him all day long about all the problems we are having. Go ahead; ask God if He would like more undivided, uninterrupted, quality time with you. I think you already know the answer.

What exactly does God want from us? That's the most important thing to consider. After all HE is the One that invited us into HIS place, right? Whenever we are invited to be a part of someone's meeting, hopefully, we don't go in with our own agenda as our focus. It should be a meeting directed by the one who set up the meeting. That's the way I see my Secret Place time.

I found when I would go in with my step one, step two, step three, mindset, I greatly hindered what God wanted to accomplish. I would leave thinking I really did something great, but later realized, it was nothing compared to what God wanted to do. I've learned to listen to Him and see what He wants for that day.

The Bible tells us to be "quick to listen, slow to speak, and slow to become angry" (James 1:19). Remember, keep things in the order they were written. Notice "listening" is first. We need to practice this in many areas of our life. Next, be slow to speak. That does not mean to s-t-a-r-t t-a-l-k-i-n-g reeeeeaaaaal sloooooow. It means don't bust in on this meeting and start talking. Listen first, and then talk. Being slow to become angry comes easy when you have done the first two things.

The order of these three things, when applied, can make a difference in many areas of our life. I do my best to apply this to my time in the Secret Place. It has made a huge difference. I feel like my prayers get answered more now than ever; and with fewer words. Interesting.

Come as you are

A lot of what I have talked about in this chapter is coming from years of experience "attempting" to dwell in the Secret Place. I use the word "attempting" because I've not always been successful. But I have never given up. I desire to spend time with my Creator. The Message Bible gives us some great advice of what to do while in the Secret Place.

Here's what I want you to do: Find a quiet, secluded place so you won't be tempted to role-play before God. Just be there as simply and honestly as you can manage. The focus will shift from you to God, and you will begin to sense his grace. "The world is full of so-called prayer warriors who are prayer-ignorant. They're full of formulas and programs and advice, peddling techniques for getting what you want from God. Don't fall for that nonsense. This is your Father you are dealing with, and he knows better than you what you need. With a God like this loving you, you can pray very simply. Like this: Our Father in heaven, Reveal who you are. (Matt. 6:6-9 MSG)

THAT is soooooooooo good! God has a "come as you are" policy in the Secret Place. It's not a "come as you think you are" policy. He wants us to be real with Him. Remember it's a REALationship with the Lord. That is our goal. Actually, God's

Secret Place policy is like this, "Come as you are, but leave as I am." I don't know about you but that stirs me up.

If a person makes their time with the Lord into a performance, a task, a works session to obtain something, or a time to submit a wish list, they will end up defeated. It's all about the relationship. It's all about time together. It's about hearts, motives, and character. It's all about walking with God in the cool of the evening as Adam did. (Gen. 3:8-10)

Two of the greatest things the Lord has given me are, a drive to be honest and transparent with both Him and people, and an almost unnatural ability to never give up. These two things have helped me so much in finding my way into the Secret Place. It's also helped me to press past the times where I felt like my time alone with God was as dry as cracker juice. Failure is not an option.

Don't ever entertain the thought that time in the Secret Place is unproductive time. I find it to be the MOST productive thing I do on any given day. You can be honest before God and you can press through and never give up. Surrender your will for God's will. He will give you the "oomph" to do it.

A lesson from my first date; seriously my very first date

When I first began spending time with the Lord, it was probably mechanical and even clumsy. It was more of a messed up scripted audition where I was trying to get hired for this relationship with Jesus. I had to work to learn how to stop trying so hard. Does that make sense? It's kind of like my first date with Margie. Get ready to laugh.

We were both in the ninth grade, probably about fifteen years old. Margie asked me out on what's called Sadie Hawkins night. That's where the girls would ask the guys out and go to dinner, the football game, and a dance afterwards. Well, she asked me out and I answered with a resounding, "Yes!" Margie was this classy, self-confident, gorgeous girl (And she still is!) and I was the no confidence, fearful, wearing blue jeans tucked into rubber work boots kind of guy.

OK, my honesty and transparency is coming out here. I was her "second" choice because the first guy already had a date; but that was fine with me. After all, this would be my first "official" date ever. I was scared to pieces but trying to "pass the audition" so to speak. As we walked up the stairs of a fancy restaurant, my lightening quick brain clicked in and thought, "Grab her arm gently and escort her up the stairs like a gentleman." Well, I guess my "aim" was off and my "gently" was a bit overbearing, because she thought I was trying to get into her purse! Yes, it's true.

Out of a normal reaction when a man "reaches" for a woman's purse, she appropriately hollered, (Note the word I chose, "hollered." It means to cry ALOUD, to SHOUT, to YELL; used to express pain or surprise or to call for help.) *"What are you doing in my purse?"* I wanted to die, and for a moment, even thought I had. I was trying to be too mechanical as if following a script! Thankfully, the Lord gave me favor because we are still together after thirty years of marriage.

It can be the same way with our time in the Secret Place. We feel as if we are the no confidence, fearful, unqualified, person with rubber boots on, coming into the holiest of holies. God asked us to come, but why in the world did He ask us? Who are we that He would be mindful of us? (Ps. 8:4) I will tell you why He invites us into "His" place. It's because He *LOVES* us! He is crazy about us... just like Margie loves me and is crazy about me! (Though it took her another year or so after that date to realize her intense love for me...)

I didn't feel like I was on the same level as Margie. We often feel that way about ourselves when it comes to God. The thing is, He doesn't feel that way at all. Don't make your time with God an audition. You are not applying for a position. You already have the position. YOU, my friend, are a child of God. Come boldly before His throne (Heb. 4:16) and enter into a REALationship, that comes from your heart. You will never be the same.

Just follow Jesus' pattern

Jesus has already set the example for us. He said He obeyed the things that His Father told Him to do. (John 14:31) He must have taken the time to listen in order to receive His instructions. Jesus did so many of these "Father initiated things" that John says, *"Jesus did many other things as well. If every one of them were written down, I suppose that even the whole world would not have room for the books that would be written" (John 21:25 NIV).*

Those "many other things" were given to Jesus by His Father. I don't think it gets any clearer. Listen to God. Hear from God. Obey God. Jesus knew His Father. He had a REALationship with Him, continually. He even pulled away from the business of life and ministry to get away and be alone with Him. If we are going to do the works Jesus has done, and even greater works according to John 14:12, then we are going to have to follow His pattern. I pray you are hungry for a REALationship with God more than ever in your life. All I can say is, "Feed that hunger!"

CHAPTER 11

The Lost Art Of Being Still

I have never been one who likes to be still. In fact, I am quite the opposite. It's not that I am hyper, I just like staying busy. Time goes by much faster when I stay busy. To me, at least the way I used to be, idle time has always been unproductive time. I'm a "task" oriented person so productivity is important.

Quite a while back, I was in the position of administrator at our church. Administration is on the low scale of what I feel my gifts are. I did whatever I could to learn more about "administrating." One day, as I was trying to improve my skills, I came across an article about high-paid executives. The article said CEO's and other top executives often appear to be time wasters. Employees would think this as they walked by the executive offices only to see them staring out a window for hours at a time. This did not seem right or fair to the employees, who are expected to always stay busy.

"Let them think!" That is the advice the article had given. The reason for this advice is the top executives are paid the big bucks to lead the entire company in the most productive and efficient way. The article said they really only make two or three major decisions per year. Yet those two or three decisions could either make or break the entire company. So, let them think their decisions all the way through. I learned right then, idle time is not always unproductive time.

Be still and know God

That one story was preparing me for yet another, life-changing principle. I would eventually apply it in my quest to get the most out of what the Secret Place offers. Even so I still had to "comprehend" that idleness could be productive. I had to learn that being still was not the same as being lazy. There is a big difference between being lazy and being still. Being lazy takes zero energy, zero effort, and produces zero results. And being lazy is definitely not productive.

Being still could well be the hardest thing that some of us have ever done. It takes effort to be still. It takes practice. It also takes something big enough to motivate a person to learn how to do this "being still." When perfected, being still is one of the most productive, creative, life altering things a person can have going for them. Especially when that person is being still in the presence of the One who created, runs, and oversees EVERYTHING! Keep reading and learn the art of being still.

The Bible says, *"Be still, and know that I am God: I will be exalted among the heathen, I will be exalted in the earth" (Ps. 46:10 King James Version).* That word "still" in Hebrew means: to slacken (in many applications, literal or figurative) to cease, relax, to let drop, to let go, to be quiet. (Strong's Concordance) God is the One speaking this verse. Therefore, what it says to me is,

Kevin, come here. Cease from your own works, let your own ideas, ways, and worries go. Be quiet and listen to me, your Creator. As you are still and quiet you get to KNOW me.

You will recognize and understand Who I AM. You will find that I am God, and you are not. Be still and let ME tell you what WE are going to do.

Oooh, I love that! I can hear God saying those exact words to me! Can you hear Him saying them to you? Go ahead and read it out loud with your name inserted in place of mine. God WANTS you to KNOW Him and being still is certainly one of the ways this can happen.

Less talk and more results

We live in an incredibly busy society. The electronic gadgets most of us own, that are supposed to save time, usually take up more time than ever. We always seem to be busy, too busy. Personally, I believe this is a well-devised scheme of the devil to get us soooooooooo busy that we have zero time to, "Be still and KNOW that God IS God."

Let's be real. Being still is NOT a popular thing these days. People used to sit on front porches and rock, and rock, and rock. I am not talking about music either. I am talking about rocking back and forth; you know, actually rock in a rocking chair. People would be alone and just sit. Imagine that.

I heard of one person who would sit in a rocker and think for hours and hours at a time. He would think, *"God, how do You run the world?"* It was said when he implemented the things God showed him throughout his life he became a very wealthy man. The whole point of this "being still" is to KNOW God. When you know God, He shares what HE knows with YOU. Now that is what I would call productive idleness.

I talk too much. Can you tell? Don't answer that. Seriously, though, especially in my prayer time, I talk too much. I can't help it. I just seem to tell God all my woes, my needs, my questions, my everything. There's nothing wrong with that, but every day? I believe there is a better way. Too often, our prayer time is us "doing business" more than it is us settling down to listen, experience, and know God. Am I saying we shouldn't pray? No. I'm saying we may need to rethink some things though.

A man in our church named Alvin is in his eighties. He is probably the most active human being in our church. On any given Sunday, he is running around (Literally!) greeting everyone. He was part of our church staff for many years, and though he's now retired, he still has a passion to encourage others beyond description. I have known him for almost thirty years now and have NEVER seen him depressed or even worried. He seems to always have a joyful "bounce" in his step and trusts God for everything.

One day I asked him for his secret to this incredible way of life. He told me he gets up every morning at about four and sits in the swing on his back porch out in the country. He may just sit there and soak up how good God is, or pray, or begin to worship God and get all caught up in it. Then he said something that changed my thinking about prayer. He said, *"Kevin, while I am sitting on the porch, worshiping God and enjoying His presence, He always sees the prayer list in my back pocket and I don't even have to pull it out! He just takes care of it!"*

Learn to settle down and do the "one thing"

Being still during our Secret Place time is us giving God a chance to do HIS thing. Not bad since His thing is life, but not just life, life more abundantly. (John 10:10) As I already said, this "being still" can end up being one of the most productive things in a person's life. It can also be the most difficult to master. Our minds and flesh go crazy when they are on "pause."

When I say be still I am not talking about an exercise of zero body movements. I am talking about a stillness of our minds, our thoughts, our to-do lists, our words, our emotions, everything. It is not as easy as it may sound but it IS possible. God would not have told us to "be still" if it were not possible.

Sometimes I will go to our church and go up to the platform and just sit there. No one is in the building. I have no agenda and really, no pre-planned words or prayers. In addition, I choose to put no limits on what God will do. I just sit there and offer myself to God. I may have a verse of Scripture in my head but that's it. I shut down everything that has to do with me so I can focus on everything that has to do with Him. It took a long, long time before I could settle down enough to do this, but it was worth the effort. At this point, I just let God be God.

So, why the wait? Why does God want us to shut it all down and be still? Do you remember in chapter seven when I mentioned the two sisters, Mary and Martha, who had received Jesus into their home for a visit? (Luke 10:38-42) Jesus was watching as Martha was running around like crazy working, cleaning, and serving. Martha got mad at Mary because Mary,

"...sat before the Master, hanging on every word he said" (Luke 10:39 MSG). She even asked Jesus to tell Mary to help her instead of just "sitting there."

Jesus replied, *"Martha, dear Martha, you're fussing far too much and getting yourself worked up over nothing. One thing only is essential, and Mary has chosen it—it's the main course, and won't be taken from her" (Luke 10:41-42 MSG).* We can all learn a lesson here. There are times when "sitting at the Master's feet" is much more important than any kind of "doing." Jesus said only one thing is essential. I think this being still helps us with our perspective of everything. We focus again. We reprioritize. We get back to the main course, the main event, the event of KNOWING God.

All the other things in life will work out when we understand the "one thing." It all works out when we understand our purpose we have been created for which is to fellowship with the Lord and KNOW He is God. Call it being still, call it quiet time, call it whatever; the key is to implement it into our time with God; and the sooner the better.

Being still is vital for a REALationship

Sometimes it's easy to wonder, "If this is a God thing so we can know Him better, then why does He make the 'being still' part so difficult?" Actually, it's not God that makes being still so difficult. It's us. With our busy lives, it seems as though we program ourselves to be in the "doing" mode. Even when we go to bed, our bodies are still yet our minds work throughout the night. We wake up worn out wondering how that could possibly be since we were sound asleep.

Well, we may have been asleep, but not "sound" asleep. In order to be "sound" asleep, we have to shut off the sounds that are constantly distracting us. And for that to happen, we have to let go of control of our lives and begin to trust God. As long as we are in control, then "we" have to solve everything. We have to figure it all out. I have learned that time in the Secret Place, getting to know God, has allowed me to trust Him. It has allowed me to trust Him totally. It has allowed me to trust Him to the point of releasing the responsibility of being in control and turning it over to Him. If God can do that in me, He can do it in you too, and He will.

Being still is a vital part of building a REALationship with God. Being still is quality, focused, undistracted time with Him that produces the REAL in this REALationship I have been talking about. Being still is such a lost art in the society we live in that it actually shows up vividly in every day life. We tend to have tunnel vision in our own little world and often don't even see it. We are so busy doing our own thing we fail to realize we have dismissed ourselves from the responsibility of building relationships. We may not see it but others sure can.

I was in an airport one time waiting on my flight. I saw a typical family of four coming down the corridor. You could tell they were a family and obviously were going on vacation; but four separate vacations. As they were walking, the dad had a newspaper in front of his face, the mom had a magazine, the son had his headphones plugged deep into his ears, and the daughter was into some kind of video game a few inches from her eyes.

As I watched, they held this pattern while skillfully navigating the heavy traffic of people; and they never even looked up. They may have been going to the same location but there was no interaction whatsoever. We have lost the art of being able to "be" without any "doing" at all. How awesome it would have been to see this family talking to one another about their trip, or holding hands, or anything at all that resembled a REALationship.

Wait! OK, now listen

When I talk about being still and knowing God I am not talking about sitting cross-legged with palms turned up, thumbs touching fingers, and going, "hmmmmm." I believe in meditation, but not that kind. I love to read a Scripture and then just be still. I sit and meditate on it. I rehearse that Scripture over, and over, and over. I sit and allow God to reveal its true meaning for my life. I listen for His voice. THAT is Godly meditation.

I don't try to tap into my inner self or anything like that. I tap into God, Jehovah God, the Almighty God. So, I sit. I wait. I sit. I wait. I wait. I listen. I listen, and I listen… not with my head, but with my heart. Sometimes I hear nothing, and that's OK. However, sometimes I hear something that must be from the Holy Spirit. I know it's directly from heaven because it is so mind-boggling there is no way it could have come from me. Like I keep saying, it's worth whatever effort it takes to know God.

Don't get me wrong, being still is not something I have totally mastered. I still have to work at turning my mind off and shutting down my to-do list. I will say this, as every year goes by it gets easier. I also find myself saying less and less in my prayer time. There is a trust we find in the Word of God that grows as we get to know the Lord. It seems like this trust, this "knowing" on the inside, begins to develop during this quality quiet time in the Secret Place. This trust, or knowing, can take a fifty word prayer request and reduce it to a four word prayer like, "Lord, I trust you."

Leaders, listen up

While working on this book I came across some interesting facts about pastors and prayer. They asked 868 active pastors throughout all fifty of the United States about their prayer life. It said, *"The ministers who are very satisfied with their prayer life spend considerably less time than average making requests, and considerably more time in quiet time or listening to God."* *(Statistics by Grey Matter Research—Phoenix, Arizona)* I think they may be onto something here.

I have found the more I get to know God, the more I seem to accomplish throughout my day. Living close definitely has its benefits. Someone said, *"Those who stay close to the throne usually only have to pray short prayers."* By being still and allowing God to download His wisdom into us we will find we have more time than ever to get things done. It's as if God knows time management like no one else... imagine that. Miraculous, truly miraculous.

Stepping out of the traffic

I have already talked about Psalms 46:10 but I want you to see it in the Message Bible. It's crazy good! It says, *"Step out of the traffic! Take a long, loving look at Me, your High God, above politics, above everything."* Is that great or what? When we rise up early, when we show up to our "appointment" with God, get alone with Him, and become still, we have stepped out of the traffic of everyday life. It's the "stepping out of the traffic" that allows us to "take a long loving look at Him." Can you imagine? US looking at HIM?

Even Moses wasn't allowed to see God all the way. You and I, through the price Jesus paid, can now come before God right into His presence. With such a privileged opportunity at hand, we need to be taking advantage of it. As I gaze upon the King of kings, I cannot picture myself doing all the talking. No wonder Isaiah 29:23 says that God's children will see how much He has blessed them and, *"...They will stand in awe of the God of Jacob" (NLT)*. I can only imagine what standing in awe of God would be like. It probably turns into an awe of silent stillness. I want to tap into that long before I get to heaven, are you up for it yet?

If I had to list all the things I feel like God has done for me during these "being still" moments in the Secret Place, there would be too many for sure. Sometimes it's not even what happens "during" the actual time frame when we are being still.

The stillness just creates a focus. It creates a putting away of our own stuff, our flesh. When we get out of the way, it allows God to be able to do what He desires.

We have to remember we are a masterpiece in the making. We may not look like it now, but once God chips away everything that doesn't look like part of his masterpiece; we will be changed into His image. We are an image that reflects God to the world. We are HIS masterpiece!

Being still allows the Lord to shine through you

Step into the revelation of Psalms 46:10. Let it become a part of your life. Let it become part of your time with God, part of your time in the Secret Place. That verse also says God will be exalted among the heathen, and He will be exalted in the earth. Notice these things happen AFTER the being still and knowing God part. It's AS we know God that we begin to see Him shine through us more than ever. The more we know Him, the less we block His light from shining through.

After a while, people won't see us, they will see Jesus IN us. They will see the Father IN us. They will see the work of the Holy Spirit as He moves THROUGH us. That is why God will be exalted in the earth. He will be able to shine THROUGH His children. The key to world evangelism is for YOU and ME to have quality, Secret Place, being still, encounters with God on a regular basis. From there, we will light up the world and dispel all darkness. Any other way is nothing more than man doing his own thing. And I think we all know that God's plan is far greater than man's plan.

Jesus said, *"The goal is for all of them to become one heart and mind—Just as you, Father, are in me and I in you, So they might be one heart and mind with us. Then the world might believe that you, in fact, sent me" (John 17:21 MSG).*

So what do you think? Are you ready to "be still and know He IS God?" Are you ready to change the world? I think you are. I can see it in your face. Wait until you see what's next....

CHAPTER 12

Crossing The Threshold

I have been working on this book at least four years or more. The majority of that time was just coming up with the chapter titles. Chapter titles are of the utmost importance. They determine the topics and set the whole tone of a book. Well, when I finally sat down to write the content of the book it had been a long time since I had looked at those chapter titles.

When I got to this chapter, "Crossing The Threshold," I had absolutely no clue as to what I meant by that. And I mean NOTHING. I even told my wife just a few days ago, *"I will probably just delete chapter twelve because I have no clue what 'Crossing The Threshold' even means."* As I sat down literally a few minutes before I am typing what you are reading right now, I felt a nudge from the Lord. I felt Him say I should at least look up the word "threshold" in the dictionary before I just delete this chapter. Obviously, I obeyed.

The first definition of the word threshold said, *"the sill of a doorway."* I'm not sure that works too well with the theme of this book. I kept reading. The second one said, *"the entrance to a house or building."* Well, with a stretch that one may work. Continuing, the third definition said, *"any place or point of entering or beginning."* Hmmm, now we may be getting somewhere. Then I looked at the fourth and last definition. It said, *"the point at which a stimulus is of sufficient intensity*

to begin to produce an effect." *(Dictionary.com)* BINGO!
Now I knew exactly why the "Lord" had me title this chapter,
"Crossing The Threshold." I knew God inspired it because I
had absolutely nothing. So, here it is, fresh off the press!

That last definition was what really got me. Crossing
the threshold is when we get to the point where our time in
the Secret Place becomes a stimulus of such intensity that it
produces an effect in us and in those around us. The minute
I read this definition God unfolded this whole chapter right
before me. I am always amazed how much God can accomplish
with a simple action of faith. That's what looking up that word
was, it was a step of faith. God moves the most when we step
out of the realm of what we can do and into the realm of what
HE can do. Remember that. It will be something you apply in
the Secret Place often.

Excitement, discipline, and passion

You see, sometimes it takes a long time before you begin
to see the effects of the Secret Place in your life. Did I say,
"Long?" I meant to say, "Looooooooooooooooong." You get the
point. It all starts with a choice, a decision. We decide we are
going to spend quality time with the Lord, not "busy" time but
quality time. Not "distracted" time or "shared" time, quality
time. We give God this time by faith. We are stepping away
from our will and into His will.

At first, it's kind of exciting; it's like a "honeymoon" for
newlyweds. As time goes by discipline is something we have to
possess. We thought we had discipline but evidently we don't.

We struggle, we fail, we start over, we rebuke the devil, and we pray for God's mercy. We want to stay consistent with this life-changing practice we read about. As we continue to press through and as we allow God to help us and change us, the flesh begins to submit. What started as a decision, became a time of excitement, then moved into discipline, but now has created a passion; a passion for time alone with God.

Passion will drive a person further than the average Christian usually ventures. You will find this passion for the Secret Place has now produced a "permanent dwelling place" where you will return day after day after day. It's when the Secret Place becomes a permanent dwelling place in our life that we can say, *"I have crossed the threshold!"* When it's no longer a retreat or a time-share but instead, a permanent residence, you have crossed that threshold. It's at this point where the desire for more of God overrules the realm of emotions, reactions, and distractions. The definition of "threshold" makes complete sense now. We are finally to the point at which a stimulus is of sufficient intensity to begin to produce an effect.

The spirit vs. the flesh

I know some of you might be saying, "Why in the world would I ever want to go through all that work of winning over my flesh?" First of all, I don't know anything of value that's easy to obtain. If Christianity were always a walk in the park then everyone would be a Christian. But know this, it's not God that makes things difficult. It's often the enemy, better known as satan, that causes trouble. Nevertheless, I have found that a big majority of troubles and roadblocks we all face are brought on by... US. Yes, you and me.

Listen, if our spirit is weak due to lack of "spiritual" feeding, we cannot blame God or the devil for that. If our flesh, our natural carnal desire, is out of control, it's not God or satan's fault. WE are the only ones who make the choices in our life. No matter what life deals to us, we are still the ones who choose what to do with those things.

When our spirit rules we are able to make right choices and push past the junk we all deal with. When ruled by our flesh it's different. Look, we all get hurt. Usually, people hurt us the most. We all get our hearts broken by others. We all feel we don't deserve to be treated that way, BUT... though we may not have been able to block those things from coming at us, we still have a CHOICE as to what we do with them. We do not have to stay hurt. We can choose to yield our broken hearts to God. We can choose to forgive those who have done us wrong... by faith. It's all about the choices we make. Now, why would we want to push through all this yuck in the world to spend this time with God? As I said before, it's because it's worth it!

The more we feed our spirit the more we walk through life the way Jesus did. The more we feed our spirit the weaker the natural side of us becomes. The fight lessens. The flesh submits. The spirit wins. It's that simple. I cannot think of a better place to feed my spirit than in the presence of God. Yes, the Secret Place is always worth the effort it takes to dwell there. When we cross that threshold, we begin to see the results. I have seen the results and I am alive because of them. Keep pressing through!

Remove, rearrange, and restore

When I began to desire to spend time with the Lord in the Secret Place it was and still is life-changing. At some point, a good number of years ago, I would find myself going to bed at night with giddiness and an excitement about getting up early the next morning. I almost didn't want to go to bed because of the anticipation for this time with God. I would wake up and quickly get ready to drive to our church. I was meeting with God!

I cannot tell you with words all He did both to me and through me during those mornings. Oh, I could tell you because I have it all written in my journals, but I can't tell you. God gets so personal with us when we allow Him to do so. He will remove, rearrange, and restore things in our lives within seconds. THAT is "crossing the threshold." Sometimes it's kind of embarrassing to find out motives and attitudes are messed up; motives and attitudes you thought you had under control. God reveals and God heals things like this in the Secret Place.

Once we find the Secret Place becoming our dwelling place we see results no human being could ever perform. Though it takes pushing through resistance, it's the pushing through that makes way for awesome results. That's why I want to be totally submitted to the Lord no matter what it takes. I want Him to fulfill all of His will in my life. I have never been disappointed in what God does in me. He is the Specialist of all specialists.

Things started happening

Looking back there was no particular "moment" where I absolutely felt I was crossing this threshold. I can't remember an exact incident where I felt so charged with sufficient intensity that this time in the Secret Place began to produce an effect. I do remember things started happening that were not initiated by me. Things like, I found myself no longer struggling to find messages to preach. The messages seemed to find me.

Things kept happening; big things! After about a seven year pursuit to know "my calling" God had the calling "find me." I could take you to the exact piece of concrete where I was standing when the Spirit of God burst on the scene to direct His purpose for my life. And the crazy thing, I was not looking for my calling or purpose at that particular time. I had given up on being so desperate for an answer. All I was doing is getting to know God. I was in hot pursuit of, "Who are You, Lord?" The Lord dropped it in my lap as if to say, *"Here is what I want you to do."*

Catch this! When you make the Secret Place your dwelling place, you will be amazed at how many things in your life fall into place. It's as if you entered into a whole new realm. It's as if you crossed the threshold into, *"a place or point of entering or beginning."*

The bride and the groom

As I thought about the title of this chapter, only one picture came to mind, a wedding. In the movies, especially the chick flicks, there is always this romantic Romeo of a man that carries his wife over the threshold. It signifies the start of their new life together. As Christians, we would say, *"the two become one" (Gen. 2:24).* Think about this for a minute. How do two become one? It's not possible. One plus one equals two. It will always equal two. Well, that's true if you are dealing with math problems, but with God, nothing is impossible. (Luke 1:37)

When two born-again Christians join their lives in marriage, they become one. God somehow makes two into one. They become forever changed. Their lives as individuals with individual goals changes into a desire to be in unity as one.

Well, I see the Secret Place in a similar way. Man has tried forever to "get to God." By their works, their doctrines, their rules, their heritage, their whatever, man has tried to get this oneness with God. It was never possible until Jesus showed up. He changed everything. Because of Jesus, we can now be one with God. When we tap into the revelation of this, and we begin to take our place in Him, we are crossing the threshold.

The best part is the groom is always the one who carries the bride INTO this new life together, this new beginning. My Bible informs me that Jesus is the groom and WE are the bride! (2 Cor. 11:2) Life gets so much better when HE carries us instead of us trying to carry ourselves.

The Body of Christ, which is you and me, is like a bride getting ready for the big day. That big day is when the groom arrives for the incredible celebration of a wedding. The groom will sweep us off our feet and carry us into our new home where all of the previous things we have been through seem like a pittance. Compared to that glorious time of spending eternity with Jesus, with our Heavenly Father, nothing we have ever experienced on earth will compare.

I don't know about you, but I am tapping into this experience early. That's what I feel happened to me when I pressed into the presence of God in the Secret Place. At some point, it was no longer about what I needed from God. It became all about Him. The decision had paid off. The discipline had paid off. The passion had paid off. Let the celebration begin! I had tapped into, *"His Kingdom come, His will be done, on earth as it is in heaven!" (Matt. 6:10)*

I know I have said this over and over but I have to say it again. Whatever it takes to make this time alone with God a regular part of your life, it's worth it. Once we cross this threshold, we don't want to go back! We are a committed bride. We have sold out to the One who swept us off our feet.

He leads us, guides us, takes care of us, loves us, and desires us. We are a treasure, which He paid a great price to acquire. He has given Himself completely to us so we have no problem giving ourselves completely to Him. Can you see it? Can you imagine it? Can you believe it? Receive it because it's true.

Since we're sold out, which means we have given ourselves completely to God, we need to stay that way. Once we start seeing what God does in our lives, there is no reason to look back. Now is not the time for looking back. We have too much ahead of us to be worrying about the past. All the "what ifs" and the "how comes" are usually futile anyway. There is no benefit in looking back. If we were to drive our cars by looking in the rear view mirror, we would end up crashing into something in front of us. We need to look ahead and allow God to navigate each one of our steps as we join Him as ONE. Aaah, that's it, perfect unity. The two have miraculously become one.

Relax, it's a wedding; enjoy the journey

Now look, this "crossing the threshold" is all about a REALationship between you and God. Be careful not to get all technical and mechanical with it. Don't start wondering things like, have I crossed it yet, am I ready to cross it, or when did I cross it? I am not trying to make a doctrine out of this. It is simply an illustration to help all of us realize the value and privilege of the amazing love God shows us. Focus on the REALationship and not on all the details.

I have officiated at many weddings in my life. Some were good and some were not. At some of the weddings, all the bridal party, the family members, and even the bride and groom are so worried about all the details that it ruins it for everyone. Even the guests sense the tension in the air. I tell them it doesn't matter if the cake falls, if the candles stay lit, if the guests are seated on the right side, if you mess up your vows, and it doesn't even matter if someone gets offended at the music. All that matters is the bride and groom saying, "I do." It's all about the couple being pronounced husband and wife.

I have also messed up several weddings all by myself. You know, mess-ups like dropping the ring, having the husband repeat the wife's vows, skipping part of the ceremony; stuff like that. Yet by the end of the service, they were married. They were officially married and entitled to cross the threshold and start their new life as one. So, don't get all bogged down with any of these details I am sharing with you. Remember, it's all about the REALationship so enjoy the journey.

A "weighty" bride

So why does it take so much time before we start to "feel" and "see" what being in the Secret Place produces? Why does this experience of crossing the threshold seem to be such a far away milestone to reach? Get ready for a unique answer to these questions. *"Ladies, please don't be offended by what I am about to say. Please!"* The worst thing I can think of, for a groom at least, before crossing the threshold would be a "weighty" bride. Weighty as in being too heavy for an easy crossing as the groom carries his bride. I know, that's not a nice thing to say but work with me. I don't want to be "overweight" with the things of this world while attempting to get into the Secret Place. I don't want Jesus to carry what He ALREADY CARRIED when He went to the cross.

There's a verse in the Bible that will help me make my point. Hebrews 12:1 says for us to, *"...lay aside the sin and*

the weights that so easily beset (clings to and entangles) us."
There have been times when I would be praying or looking up a
Scripture while in the Secret Place, when God would interrupt
me and say, *"I want you to forgive so-and-so."* I'm like, "Where
did that come from?" Not only that, God would also deal with
me to pray for them and bless them. What was He doing? God
was helping me "burn off that extra weight" I had carried into
the Secret Place. He wanted me to let go of anything that would
get in between us. The weights of worry, fear, bitterness, sin,
selfishness and the like will leave if I choose to let them go. He
had already carried them "for me" so I could freely enjoy my
time with Him.

God doesn't expect us to do this on our own. That's why He
gave us a Savior; Jesus Christ. We do have the responsibility
of responding to what He says though. Obedience is better than
sacrifice. (1 Sam. 15:22) Our time in God's presence doesn't
really matter if that time is spent in disobedience to His desires.
Leave it all behind. It's too heavy to carry around. And the
Groom has already provided the healthy food of His Word and
whatever else we need to shed this "extra weight." Just receive
what He has and follow the instructions. We will all be pleased
with the results.

We were created for this

There is something that happens when we do a particular
thing long enough that it becomes a part of us. This is certainly
true about the Secret Place. Eventually it becomes natural to
us. It can even cross our mind that "we were created for this."

Though it was awkward in the beginning, when that threshold is finally crossed, it all makes sense. Something we didn't fully understand becomes something we can't live without.

When we cross the threshold and allow this time with God to be "what we do" we are stepping into what we were created for. Getting to know God is supposed to be such a part of us that we don't struggle with it, we don't freak out about it, and we aren't scared of it. It's simply what we do. The Creator designed us to have this intimate fellowship with Him. As we continue to allow it to be a part of our lives, this supernatural God we serve will make hanging out with Him as natural as breathing. It's what we do.

As we pursue the life-changing tangible presence of God, we will always see results. Yes, it may take a little longer than we want, but what's new? After all, we live in a fast-food microwave world where patience is more of an endangered species than a virtue. I have found that even though we may be in the last of the last days on earth, God is not in a hurry.

God knows it takes time to carve out a masterpiece. He is carving out a masterpiece He can and will use for His glory. Don't be discouraged with the building process. The results will amaze all of us. The beauty of a "reflection of Christ" is magnificent. We are a reflection in the making. Don't get off the Potter's wheel before He is finished. Revel in the reality that each one of us is destined to be one with The One. Welcome to a REALationship with the Lord!

CHAPTER 13

Behind Closed Doors

By now, I pray you really do have a desire to get alone with God on a regular basis. Jesus paid a heavy price for us to have this incredible privilege and we shouldn't neglect it. When God gives us opportunities as great as meeting with Him in the Secret Place we can certainly know it's for a reason. God always has a plan. His plans are designed to produce a desired outcome. Though I don't know everything God desires to accomplish in this intimate time with Him, I do believe He has given me at least "some" insight as to the purpose of these regular times with Him.

As you read this chapter, step out of the natural way of thinking and hear from the Spirit of God as He places things into your spirit. Allow the Spirit of God to "impart" something to you as you read. And yes, once again, this truth of "Behind Closed Doors" did change my life. Are you counting how many times I have said that?

When you pray

We find the thought of "behind closed doors" in Matthew 6:6 where Jesus is instructing His disciples and others who had gathered on a mountain. He had just told them not to pray as the hypocrites do. They prayed these real eloquent prayers in public so everyone could see how spiritual they were. He continues when He says, *"But you, when you pray, enter into your room. And shutting your door, pray to your Father in secret; and your Father who sees in secret shall reward you openly" (Matt. 6:6 MKJV).*

I know we mentioned this verse in chapter ten, but now I want to do more than just mention it. If you look at it a little closer you will see that Jesus gives us some great spiritual instructions for the Secret Place.

The first thing Jesus says is, *"But you, when you pray..."* I take that to mean He already believes we are going to pray. Otherwise, He would have said, "If you pray." Prayer is not an option for Christians. After all, what is prayer? Prayer is communicating with God. It's this communication with God that we build our lives from.

Jesus also told the people, *"When you pray... enter into your room."* Other translations say things like, go into your most private room, go away by yourself, find a quiet place, or go into your closet. The picture here is to "get away somewhere in a quiet place all by yourself." I know I have used my actual closet before. Others sit on their back porch, retreat to another room in the house, go to a church sanctuary, or sit by themselves in some scenic place. The key is to find somewhere you can be in a quiet and peaceful setting. Creativity dwells in tranquility. It's kind of hard to focus on communicating with God if we are in a place where the noise of life is overbearing.

Make sure you shut the door

Once we are in that quiet place it's time to "shut the door." Shutting the door simply means turning off and shutting out every distraction. This is what I have been talking about throughout this book. Jesus sets the example and gives direct instructions that show us the Father desires our undivided attention. He wants our best. He doesn't want to be in competition with other things in order to have this undivided attention with us.

While on staff at our church, I stressed out one summer due to the fact we had scheduled a soccer camp and had no one to teach it. We were desperate to find someone who could help us because time was running out. So I told the church secretary I would be busy for at least an hour. I was heading into the sanctuary to meet with God about the soccer dilemma we were facing.

As I was up at the altar pleading my case before God I felt a little nudge on the inside. That nudge was the Lord. He said, *"Do you really need your cell phone when you are talking to me?"* I reminded Him I was hoping someone would call in response to all my requests to find someone for this camp. That didn't go over at all. I ended up not only turning it off but taking it to the farthest pew so I wouldn't even be tempted to check it.

God wanted me. He didn't want me with all the stuff I carried in. He wanted me. He wanted time alone with the uninterrupted, undivided, distraction free, Kevin. I submitted and gave Him what He desired. I gave Him my best. I had shut the door.

When I came out of the sanctuary, there was a note on my office door that the secretary had left. A soccer coach had called from Dallas. He didn't know me and I didn't know him. I had not called him or the college where he worked. This man wanted to know if I would be interested in having two ex-pro soccer players from Brazil come and do a soccer camp for FREE. You can only imagine how thrilled I was. Not only had God provided but He provided the very best in a supernatural way.

All it took was me entering into that private and secluded place and shutting the door. Did my powerful and anointed prayers convince the Lord to answer my prayers? No, not at all. God KNEW what I needed before I even asked Him. (Matt. 6:8) All that had to happen was for me to enter into the Secret Place undistracted. God was able to settle me down from all the stress I had put on myself. Once at peace, I could cease from "my works" and enter into "His work." I had tapped into the Almighty God who "sees" in secret.

God sees "in secret" and rewards "openly"

As human beings, we typically see in color. They say that animals see in black and white. I really don't know how they can say that seeing how the animals can't exactly tell us what they see. Regardless, we see in color while others see in black and white. God sees different from us. He sees in "secret." Matthew 6:6 says, *"...pray to your Father in secret; and your Father who sees in secret shall reward you openly."*

This does not mean there is a room called "secret" and that is the only place God can see. It simply means that when a person is making it a point to spend quality time with God,

He notices that. He takes note of it and there is a reward for it. It's not a reward based on works. It's a reward based on the fact that we made time with Him a priority in our life. We took time out of our day to honor Him with one of the most valuable assets on earth; TIME.

This is why I am such a believer in the Secret Place. So much happens while we are alone with God a person could write a book on it. A person cannot remain the same if they will make time in the Secret Place a part of their daily routine. Blessings, favor, and a whole host of other things are the rewards of this time. Those soccer players were rewards. They were not a reward because I did something or earned something. Any loving Father would reward their child who honors, respects, and spends quality time with them.

I don't think someone is cursed if they don't spend time alone with the Lord. I just think they live far below the level of life they've been created to live. I do not want to miss out on anything God has for me. Call it selfish but I want everything He has to offer.

With many airlines today, there are frequent flier programs that offer "miles" and "rewards." If we fly enough to gain a certain amount of miles, we get the reward of a free upgrade or a free ticket. Not a bad deal, right? If a person has to fly then why not earn miles while flying, especially when there is a reward for it. Technically, the miles and rewards are not "earned." The person was already flying anyway. The extra bonus to gain free miles is a perk, an added blessing.

That's the Secret Place. I never go into the Secret Place to gain rewards. Nevertheless, while I am in the Secret Place, if the One who sees in secret wants to add some rewards, I am all for it. Did I earn these rewards? No, but the bonus when we are faithful and loyal members of the right carrier is wonderful. "Oh Lord, help us all to be faithful and loyal to the greatest carrier ever; Jesus Christ."

What goes on behind closed doors?

Can you handle a bit more? I want to take this message of the Secret Place to a completely new level in the next few moments. It may take a few paragraphs to give the whole picture so press through until I am finished.

I remember one of my times in the Secret Place. It was during that time period when I was setting my alarm extremely early every morning. The excitement of what God was doing in my life was incredible. On this particular day, I was really focusing on Matthew 6:6. I wanted to make sure I had "shut the door" and was not allowing myself to be distracted by my to-do list, my own thoughts, or anything concerning myself. I wanted to focus on the Master who holds the world in His hands.

After taking this verse of Scripture and reading it over and over again, the Lord spoke a clarity that could only mean, "Get ready for this." He asked me, *"Kevin, in the natural, what goes on behind closed doors?"* I was rather taken back by that question. Having read Matthew 6:6, what seemed like a million times, I kind of knew what the answer was. I answered the Lord, *"Well, I guess intimacy between a married couple takes place behind closed doors if we are talking about the natural realm."* Then something clicked, *"Reproduction takes place behind closed doors. Is that the answer, Lord?"*

In those next few moments' revelation flowed like a river. Not only does reproduction take place, but what develops is something that is born in the likeness and the image of the husband and wife. It's a true "reproduction" of themselves which can be proven all the way down to the DNA.

Now, I had a question for the Lord. *"What in the world does THAT have to do with the Secret Place?"* The Lord shared with me about the importance of an intimate relationship with Him in the Secret Place. When we get alone with the Lord, and we are behind closed doors, there is something "spiritual" that takes place. I am not talking about natural things. I am talking spiritual things. (Don't get all freaked out about this. This is spiritually speaking.)

All of us are called to "make disciples of all people." (Matt. 28:19-20) The way to "reproduce" true disciples of the Lord is for us to be with Him. HE is the only One who can give someone the desire to follow Him. We do the sharing and talking and inviting, but HE is the One who pulls at their heart. As each of us becomes one with the Lord, we will be "fruitful" because of Him. It won't be because of our clever discipleship programs or our new believer's classes. There is nothing wrong with those things. I have taught them many times. But to make disciples that last, something has to be birthed by the Spirit of

God. God must be involved from the beginning… especially since He IS the beginning.

When the two become one

When the Lord gave me this revelation, I was the youth pastor at our church. He told me the greatest thing I could ever do to grow the youth group was to spend plenty of time in the Secret Place. That way, when I preached, or when I trained leaders, or set up a discipleship program, it would be something that CAME OUT OF the Secret Place; the Secret Place where reproduction BEGINS.

We cannot do this task of winning the world for Jesus WITHOUT HIM. The TWO have to become ONE. Jesus was, and still is, one with the Father and He is our example to follow. We become one with Him when we, *"…enter into your room. And shutting your door, pray to your Father in secret; and your Father who sees in secret shall reward you openly."*

There are too many things we do as Christians that are well meaning good things but they are not God things. Remember, Jesus said He ONLY did that which His Father told Him to do. (John 14:31) Everything Jesus accomplished came out of the time He spent with His Heavenly Father. If that's how Jesus did it, then that's how we must do it. The reason I said at the beginning of this book, *"I believe anything and everything can be found in the Secret Place,"* is because that's where it all begins.

Please don't think I am saying if you haven't spent time with God on any given day then you can't be used by Him.

I am not saying that at all. I'm saying in order for us to be as productive and as effective as possible, what we do for the Lord needs to flow out of our relationship with Him. We bear "much" fruit when we follow the pattern of Jesus when He said, *"I am the vine; you are the branches. If a man remains in me and I in him, he will bear much fruit; apart from me you can do nothing" (John 15:5 NIV).*

You become like the one you hang out with the most

When I realized the overwhelming importance of spending time in the Secret Place, it changed everything. With the message Jesus spoke in Matthew 6:6 it brought time with God to the top of my priorities. As we put God first, and are willing to show it by investing time to build a relationship with Him, we will see results. We will bear fruit. That's what happens behind closed doors; spiritual reproduction, otherwise known as, "making disciples of all nations."

I read a secular statistic once that said be careful who you hang around with. It said a person would end up becoming like the top five people they are with the most. It finished by saying you had better take a good look at these five people in your life because chances are, you will end up just like them. Now, I am not sure how they came up with that and I am not sure if it's all totally accurate. I do know the Bible says everything reproduces after its own kind. (Gen. 1:11)

That being the truth, I want to hang around the Lord as much as possible so I can be a reflection or a product of Him. As I take on His image, people won't see me; they will see Him through me. People will see that I have been with Jesus. (Acts 4:13) THAT is what true disciples are because it all starts with Jesus. You cannot emanate Jesus without producing something good; yet another reason to master our time with the Master.

To me, Matthew 6:6 sums up the how to and the why of the whole concept of the Secret Place. It tells us we are to pray. It tells us to go to a quiet and secluded place. It tells us to shut the door on distractions so we can focus on the Lord. It even encourages us by telling us God sees in secret. The world may not see what we accomplish in the Secret Place but God certainly does. God will reward us openly because He is so good. He loves to bless His children who get to know Him. Does God get mad at us if we don't take advantage of this time in the Secret Place? No, but I would guess He probably misses us.

CHAPTER 14

Jump-Start Your Journal

Before I even start this next topic, I need to say something to the men who are brave enough to actually read a chapter on journaling. First off, guys, thanks for reading this chapter. Second, keep an open mind as you continue to read. I promise you will live through it and you might even apply it to your life. Just keep one thing in mind, anything God speaks is worth writing down. I am always prepared to write because I expect God to talk to me all the time. How about you?

OK, back to everyone. A journal is simply defined as: a daily record, as of occurrences, experiences, or observations. Here's my definition: A journal is something a person creates in the present, to read in the future, in hopes to learn and be encouraged by things written in the past. You might have to read that again to let it soak in. It's actually profound. That one statement describes my journal perfectly.

A journal?

I have many hand-written journals I have filled during my Secret Place time. I also have thousands of devotions I have written in something I call, The E-quip Devotion. (Sign up for this free devotion at: PastorKevin.com) Every journal entry and devotion is a daily record of occurrences, experiences, and observations that emerged from my Secret Place time with God. I don't feel like these things were written because I am a writer. They were written to record the daily inspiration that comes with daily time in the Secret Place. They were written because everything God shows us is worth writing down.

The journals, the devotions, and even this book are products of the Secret Place. I have some entries that are, *"thus saith the Lord"* kind of stuff and others that are observations and experiences. Put them all together and you have something called journaling. I don't consider my journals a diary. I know they are basically the same thing. I guess that word "diary" doesn't sit with me as good as the word "journal" does. Oh well, it's probably a guy thing. Call it what you want but the point is to do it.

It was in August of 1999 when the Lord spoke to me to start The E-quip Devotion. At that time I knew absolutely nothing about computers. Evidently, that didn't keep the Lord from telling me these devotions were to go out in the form of e-mails. A friend of mine showed me the basics of "computerism" and I actually learned how to "do" e-mail from an AOL picture book. As crazy as that seems, it was another turning point in my life.

I had been writing in a notebook concerning things the Lord would show me while alone with Him. The E-quip Devotion took those kinds of entries to a different level. When the Lord dealt with me about writing these daily devotions, He gave me two distinct and specific instructions. He told me to, "Never ask Him ahead of time (or anytime for that matter) what I was to write about." He then instructed me to "Type (or write) out of the overflow AFTER I had spent time with Him… He would provide the material if I would provide the time alone with Him." Wow!

After thousands of devotions, many books of journal entries, and now the book you are reading, I still follow those two instructions from God. Every page in this book was written AFTER my time with God. I am not bragging about this, I am just showing you the faithfulness of God. Time with God always produces fruit. This book was birthed out of time with the Father. Once again... Anything and everything can be found in the Secret Place!

It's more than just a few words in a notebook

Most everything I write is a daily account of what the Lord shows me on that particular day. What really sold me on journaling was when I looked back at my old entries and my old devotions. It's like looking into my past and seeing all the incredible things God has done in my life. From the tests and troubles I talked about to the triumphs and victories, it's all there.

When I get frustrated, discouraged, or even depressed, I often go back and read about the things God has done in me. I read several of my journal entries and the verses that I wrote about. I read all the things I've written of God's faithfulness; how He pulled me through once again. By the time I read ten or twenty of those I become encouraged and ready to take on the world. This is a perfect example of that statement I made at the beginning of this chapter, "A journal is something a person creates in the present, to read in the future, in hopes to learn and be encouraged by things written in the past."

Do you remember when our teachers would have us write out all the sentences over and over when we were learning how to write? For years, you could probably quote the exact sentences you had used in your learning. If you are old enough it would be something like, "See Spot run." Why are those sentences still with us? It's because there is something that happens when we write things out. It's the same way with Scripture. When I write Scriptures down a few times they seem to stick with me more than when I just read them. The act of writing something down has been helpful in imprinting that moment or Scripture on my brain and in my heart.

As we purpose to write about what the Lord shows us while we are with Him, two things happen. It helps us to remember those things He speaks to us, which allows us to share them with others. Then, as we go back and actually read our past entries, it reminds us of how awesome God is. We read those things and say, *"Man that had to be God! I could have never come up with something like that."* It turns our focus right where it needs to be, which is on God. HE gets glory when we review all the great things He has done in our lives.

When God speaks, it's always worth writing down

Because I believe the things God shares with us are worth writing down, I try to be prepared. I not only believe the Lord speaks to us, I expect it. So, I want to be ready at all times. I had to start keeping pen and paper at my bedside. I've even woken up and typed myself a note on my cell phone. I have my iPad at my bedside now, but whatever it takes, that's what I say.

There are some mornings I wake up and hear something from the Lord before I even get out of bed. It's as if God was hovering over me just waiting for me to wake up. As soon as my eyes open, He immediately says something profound. I have to write it down so I won't forget it. I have also learned the hard way that I can't always remember it without writing it down. I have had too many things from the Lord slip out of reach, only to be forgotten, due to my laziness or procrastination to write it down. "A revelation that slips away quickly turns into a realization to never let it happen again!"

For the most part, I take notes and write down things the Lord reveals to me during my Secret Place time. If for some reason I cannot write it at that moment, then I write it down shortly afterwards. I want what I write to be fresh. The key to this is to be prepared. If we REALLY believe the Lord will speak to us, then we need to have actions that show we believe.

Many times we think we have nothing to write about. Our reasoning is, *"God never says anything to me."* Do you remember how I said God didn't want me asking Him what to write about in the devotions? He was training me to "expect" Him to show me things. He wanted me to put actions behind those expectations by being prepared to write. Faith without action or works is dead. (James 2:17) It showed God I really believed He would speak to me by showing up in the Secret Place with a journal and a pen.

That may sound silly but according to "our" faith it is done unto us. (Matt. 9:29) We show God respect and honor when we are prepared to write down whatever He says. By doing this we are saying, *"I not only believe you are going to speak to me but I also think what you say is important enough to write down."* As we honor Him with this simple task we will see more and more revelation in our lives.

The Lord has shown me so many things. Is it because I am a preacher, or smart, or better than someone else? No, of course not. It's simply because I showed up in the Secret Place and was prepared to listen. Simple things with faithfulness go a long way with God. Journaling is a simple thing, yet when acted upon diligently is completely life changing.

So many ways to journal

My hand written journals are just empty books with lines in them until I fill them. I used to buy cheap spiral notebooks, which I'm sure is fine. One day I decided to upgrade to something better because these journals were about "God encounters." I wanted to use something that would last longer and seem a bit more appropriate to hold such life changing material. I bought inexpensive notebooks (usually made of fake leather but they look nice) that still look good today after all these years. I have several that are still waiting for me to fill them.

Now that I am an official computer geek, I use software on my laptop (Advanced Diary: www.csoftlab.com/Diary. html) or iPad. It made sense because that's where all my Bibles and study tools are located. This allows me to have several different journals and the ability to organize and print them out if necessary. And of course, every devotion I write is a journal of my time with God so I paste them into my digital journal as well. It's so easy to find years of entries with just a click or two.

It doesn't matter how you journal the things God shows you. It just matters that you do it. Personally, when I moved from the hand written notebook to the laptop, I liked the laptop better. Whenever I travel though, I always have a leather bound notebook I carry with me. I do this because I may not always be in front of my laptop when God speaks. I have one of those notebooks in the glove box of my car, one in my office, and I have extras in my desk in case I need them.

I am THAT serious about this. All I can tell you is God has certainly honored it. So, use a hand written journal, a laptop with journal software (Or without it. It's just easier with it.), your mobile phone, a pocket recorder, whatever, but do it. Whatever you use just make sure you are able to save all your entries. It doesn't matter if you save them on a bookshelf or on a hard drive, just save them. Someday, as you reflect over them, you will be thrilled you did. It is so cool to go back and read them all. God has been so good to me. He has been good to you too, you just may have forgotten "how good" if you didn't write it down. Hint hint…

Writing turns to revelation

When I write in my journal, it might be just a few words or it might be several pages. All I am doing is giving God the opportunity to trust me with another nugget of His truth. Some people write every single thought they have and some only write the highlights. I don't think there is a right or a wrong way to do it. Just do it.

What exactly do I write? I write on what I read in the Word of God that day. I write about how I feel towards the Lord. I write how He feels about me. I even write things the Lord deals with me about concerning surrender, repentance, love, patience, or anything else. The main thing is to write from your heart not just your head. Remember, it's not just any ol' relationship, it's a REALationship.

And if you are still asking yourself, "Why do all this?" then listen up. As you are writing, you are sealing it in your heart. And not only that, but when you begin to write what you thought was a revelation, it ends up exploding with even more revelation. When we receive what the Holy Spirit gives us, it creates an atmosphere for more. Before long, the person who felt like God never speaks to them is writing more than they can fit in their journal.

If someone were to ask me, "What is the one tip you can give me that will help me be a success at journaling?" My answer would be, "Write by faith." Let me explain what I mean by that. Whenever I preach at a church, I normally have some notes about the message. I also rarely share what I am preaching on before I preach it. I want to make sure I deliver the message as God gave it to me, not with someone's opinion mixed in. If that sounds rude it's not meant to. It's just the way it is for me.

It never fails, "as" I am preaching from my notes, I begin to speak things that are obviously from the Lord. As I am speaking about something I've written in my notes, God reveals things you cannot find in my notes. It is awesome! It's as if I am learning things at the same time I am preaching them. Well, it's the same way with journaling. Hundreds and even thousands of times I have written one thing and God adds to that one thing... as I am writing! If I hadn't written down what I do know, in faith, then I would not have tapped into what I didn't know. Are you getting this?

How can something like this happen? Ask God, not me. HE is the One that does it. I know faith pleases God. (Heb. 11:6) He gets so much pleasure out of us honoring Him enough to write it down (by faith) that He just leans over to the Holy Spirit and says, *"Go ahead, give them some more; show them how big We are!"* Write down those thoughts He gave you. Who knows, you may have a book before you know it.

Journaling during tough times

Some of my greatest entries I have made in my journal were when I was in a time of severe pain from that fall down the stairs I told you about. During all those years of severe pain... excuse me, SEVERE PAIN, the Lord told me to do things by faith. He told me to never turn down or cancel a speaking engagement due to pain. I will tell you right now that was the hardest thing ever. There were times where Margie would literally have to help me to the car after preaching because the pain was so great.

For a while, the severe pain kept me out of the Secret Place. I wouldn't sleep at night so therefore I couldn't get up early like I normally would. When I did get up, there was a whole regimen of things that had to be done just to walk or get dressed. It was horrible. Finally, I realized I had to get back to the Secret Place, regardless of the pain or the struggle it would take to accomplish the task. You see, I believe what I am telling you in this book. The Secret Place is not a "story" I am sharing with you. It's an experience I believe in; it's a major part of my life. In fact, it's where I find life; the life only Jesus can supply.

It was during those times of suffering when I went to my Secret Place totally by faith. The sacrifice, the effort, the pain of enduring every single step was all worth it. I received revelation and help from God I never dreamed possible. Try to catch the atmosphere and the passion I was experiencing when you read a few of my entries over the next several pages. I am sharing these intimate and personal things with you so you will have an example of a journal entry. You will see just how real these Secret Place appointments can be. Remember, these are straight from my journal with no editing or polishing; they are straight from the heart.

A few of my own personal journal entries

September 30, 2004 – *The peace and the presence of God that I feel in the Secret Place, in these early morning hours, is the greatest thing ever. Words cannot describe the "Welcome!" I feel from the Heavenly Father, Himself. It's as if He is waiting for me to come through that door. No sermon, no amount of money, no person, and no job, no anything can make me feel the way I feel in the Secret Place. I have found the "Pearl of great price" and I don't ever want to lose it. I know it's only by the grace and the mercy of God that I have been able to get up early and come down here to meet with the Lord. "Please Lord, let it NEVER end!" I don't ever want to go back to sleeping late and missing what God has for me in the Secret Place. Thanks be unto God for placing me in the Secret Place with Him. May my time with Him in this place increase and deepen. I have barely scratched the surface. "Help me Lord, to dig for more!"*

October 05, 2004 – *God is causing there to be a work in my heart that cannot survive without the Secret Place. I love that! I know only God could be doing this. That simply is NOT me. To be so desirous of the Secret Place that you become frantic when the thought of not having time there can only be God. That is something I have longed to have for years! "Thank You, Jesus! Please don't stop! Keep drawing me to the place where I cannot live without You, Lord!"*

As I see that the Lord is really working a work in me that goes beyond words I am greatly humbled and in awe. The fact that he would do this for me is the greatest thing ever. I have longed to have a heart that longs for Him! He is doing that. No man can do that. When I preach about the Secret Place and intimacy with God, I cannot MAKE people get it. That is something that ONLY the Holy Spirit can do. "Holy Spirit, please use me as a vessel that You can flow through to tell others about the Secret Place. And then, confirm Your Word with signs following. Draw them into the Secret Place the way You are drawing me. Please Lord, let this happen!"

I think, we as Christians, have some things concerning intimacy with God and the Secret Place mixed up; confused. Having a "prayer life" is NOT to be compared to "intimacy with God" no more than "having sex" should be compared to "intimacy with your spouse." They are completely different! I think because we pray for our kids, our ministry, our church, our president, etc., we think we have had intimacy with God. Well, that's simply NOT true! Intimacy with God often requires no words. Sometimes it requires no talking about others. It requires privacy, total attention, passion, and your heart. It's NOT something that you just DO. Sometimes we just "say" our prayers. It's something we DO. It's not passionate or personal the way intimacy in the Secret Place is. Like I said, there is a BIG difference. I have a feeling the more time we spend being intimate with God, the less "wordy" our prayers will become. I think Jesus' life shows this. He had intimacy with His Heavenly Father, yet, sometimes His "prayers" were only a few or even one sentence long. So, instead of praying a lot, to get the desired results and calling that intimacy, let's spend time in the Secret Place and allow that intimacy to produce prayers and results. There are many benefits and *results that come from intimacy with God. Just look at Psalms 91 for example. The first sentence tells us to "dwell in that Secret Place" but then it spends the rest of the chapter telling you about all of the results and benefits that will come out of the "Secret Place."..........More time in the Secret Place equals less time in prayer. Wow!*

October 06, 2004 *– The very thing that motivated me to dive into the Secret Place like never before is no longer what motivates me. At first, I dove in because of the whole "back pain" syndrome I was experiencing. It was, for lack of better words, a HEALTH thing. But, NOW the thing that draws me and motivates me to get up very early each day is a relentless longing to be with my Heavenly Father! Words cannot come close to describing what I feel the moment I "step into" the Secret Place. I absolutely long and yearn to be in His presence. Nothing that I do throughout my entire day even compares to my time with the Lord. When it's time to go to work, I immediately start longing for the next morning. This can ONLY be God that is doing this in me! All I can say is, "Thank You, Lord!" "You have been sooooooooooo good to me!" I have spent many years praying and reading my Bible, but this is different. This is so intimate, so personal, and so deep. The Bible springs to life. My prayers are those of praise and adoration more than they are of requests and petitions. What is so funny, is realizing just how much there is in our life that is NOT important when it's compared to spending intimate time with God. What is it that would be more important in my life than sitting down and having a face-to-face talk with the Lord? And I cannot picture myself walking past Jesus saying, "Sorry Lord, I have something else that I really need to go do." No way could I* *do that! Yet, I have done that for YEARS! "Father, forgive me for letting so many things become more important than "time with You!" So what is it that is making this current time in the Secret Place so different than any other time over the last 25 years? Is it the "location" of "where" I am praying? No. I could be in my closet, in my truck, at home, up here at the church, or anywhere. Here is what it is: It's the LOCATION of my HEART! Blessed are the "poor" in spirit. God is looking for that broken and contrite heart. THAT is the difference! Sometimes it takes years of TROUBLE in our lives to get us to the point where absolutely NOTHING is more important than our time with God. It certainly took many years for me!*

Oh, and by the way, it's not God's fault that it takes so long to achieve the right kind of heart. It's my own fault. I am the one that kept putting everything else before Him. It was ME that kept putting "the ministry" more important than time with the One who gave me the ministry. I didn't do it on purpose, but nevertheless, I did it. I can only pray it will NEVER happen again. As long as I spend time in the Secret Place it will not matter how I preach. In other words, whether I preach illustrated cool sermons for the youth or straight and monotone, it will not matter. Why? It's NOT the "preacher" that makes things happen during a service. It's God! And when the "preacher" has been with Jesus, then THAT will be enough and people will be able to SEE that we have been with Him. It's not how the preacher delivers his message that causes results. It's where he's been (or hasn't been) that causes results. Has he been in the Secret Place? It is so easy to get all of this confused and out of whack. Currently, my time in the Secret Place never seems to be long enough. It's too short! I want more! But, I guess that's good. That keeps me hungry for more. If I were to be satisfied then I wouldn't have anything drawing me back for more...

One more thing... get started!

Whatever it takes, learn to journal. The benefits far outweigh the struggles. Seems I have said that somewhere else in this book already. It's so true though. Journaling takes time. It takes effort. It takes discipline. But, it also takes you to a whole new level. I cannot explain to you what happens when I read those entries I wrote during those painful years with back trouble. I can feel the agony and the anguish I was in when I wrote them.

What I also feel is the great praise to a faithful God who brought me through all those hard times. I am so encouraged when I look back and see how far God has brought me. No one will ever know the depth of the mental and physical healing the Lord provided for me. I am so glad I have it in print so when new trials come, I can go back and see the victories God has given me. I follow David's example by saying something like, *"With God's help, I have killed the lion, I have killed the bear, and I will do the same to this giant before me.........and I have the written proof in my journals to show it!!!" (1 Sam. 17:36)*

So, there you have it! You know as much about journaling as I do. Now all you have to do is "do it." Make the choice, add the action, and see the results. Allow me to say this one last time, *"YOUR journal is something you create in the present, to read in the future, in hopes to learn and be encouraged by things written in the past."* You can do it!

CHAPTER 15

Dive In!

Well, we're here! Hopefully, you didn't just flip to the last chapter and read it first. If so, turn the pages all the way back to the beginning and start there. This is not a book a person can figure out by reading the first and last chapter. Now, if you did actually read the whole book then know this, *"I am soooooooooo PROUD OF YOU!"* I mean that with all my heart. This chapter is written especially for you!

Focus on the destination instead of the difficulty of the journey

I've found the Secret Place is not always the most popular topic for Christians. I think it's because it requires something from them. That "something" is action; better known as obedience, discipline, prioritizing and follow through, you know bad words like those. As humans, we don't usually like to read or hear about things that require something of us. We would rather read about other people's determination and discipline, but only if they don't include us in it. We usually want the road of least resistance.

The road of least resistance has one major flaw with it though. That flaw is found in Matthew 7:13. It talks about two gates, two roads. The narrow gate with a narrow road leads to life. Only a few choose that one. But many choose the easier gate, after all it's easy. It's described as a wide gate, a wide road. The wide gate leads to destruction. The people that follow the wide road never enter into the life that the narrow road brings. I love the way this is portrayed in the Message Bible.

Don't look for shortcuts to God. The market is flooded with surefire, easygoing formulas for a successful life that can be practiced in your spare time. Don't fall for that stuff, even though crowds of people do. The way to life--to God!—is vigorous and requires total attention. (Matt. 7:13-14 MSG)

Thankfully, people like yourself don't care as much about the road as you do about where that road leads you. You are concerned about the DESTINATION, not the difficulty it may take to get there. You must be a "total attention" kind of person since you are reading the last chapter of this book. I can tell you want life regardless of the struggle it may take in order to get there. You aren't doing it to be seen or to be popular. You are doing it because it's right. It's right according to the Word of God. That narrow road is plenty wide for people like you who are willing to step out of the boat and walk on the water by faith.

Others may be satisfied to "see" someone walk on water, but not you or me. We are determined to know what it "feels" like to walk on water. What it looks like is not enough for us. We want to experience it. Like I said, I am sooooooooo proud of you! Let's DIVE IN!!!

Dive in... even if you feel a little clumsy

What do I mean when I say dive in? Well, I mean get started. Don't wait until you have it all figured out. Step into the Secret Place by faith. Even if you stumble around and feel clumsy with it, do it anyway. Focus on building this REALationship with your Heavenly Father.

The first time I went "soul winning" with a team of people from our church was a scary yet funny experience for me. This was before I had ever preached or anything like that. I was still new in the things of God but I wanted to tell someone about Jesus. We went to a shopping mall to share Jesus with anyone who would listen. My friend had told me how to approach people and how to share the Lord with them. I was terrified! No, you don't understand, I was terrified, scared, fearful, and nervous. It was a sick to my stomach kind of nervous. Nevertheless, I was determined so I pressed through.

After waiting for a perfect set up, which never came, I finally decided I would have to "make" myself do this. So, I stood at the bottom of an escalator and made up my mind to talk to the next person who came down. Wouldn't you know it, a big construction worker kind of guy got on the escalator. I was so scared he almost had to knock me out of the way to keep from getting sucked under the moving stairs.

Anyway, I made my way through my "Gospel presentation outline" with this man and he actually listened. I botched up the Gospel like no one had ever done before. I probably told the man that Jesus was raised from the dead before I ever told him about His death on the cross. I was THAT nervous. To my surprise, the guy gave his life to the Lord right there at the bottom of that escalator. I led him through a prayer, which I really messed up as well, and he surrendered his life to Jesus. He was so touched that when his wife walked up he immediately told her what he had done with big ol' tears in his eyes.

Why the long story? It's not all about us. I messed up royally that day. I stumbled. I was clumsy with my presentation. But it wasn't about me, it was about a soul coming to know Jesus. It's the same way with diving into the Secret Place. It may feel awkward. It may be difficult at first. But it's not about you... yet.

It's about a REALationship with your Heavenly Father. It's about His desire to see you and to spend time with you. It's about satisfying God's desire. He doesn't mind the clumsiness or the seeming lack of what to say or do. All that matters to God is that YOU, His creation He is well pleased with, showed up to meet with Him. I know He smiles as you enter this Secret Place by faith. Give it time. Your Secret Place will eventually become your dwelling place.

It starts with a decision not a feeling

Dwelling in the Secret Place is a choice. It all starts with a decision. You don't have to wait for a confirmation from an angel. You don't have to wait until you feel it. You just make the decision, *"I am going to start spending quality time with the Lord in the Secret Place on a regular basis."* That's all it takes. If a person waits for a feeling they will have a hard time continuing when there aren't any feelings.

I always have to go back to a marriage as my example. Eventually, the excitement of a honeymoon wears off. It's hard to be "honeymoon-ish" when all the wife and husband have dealt with that day is poopy diapers, snot, harsh bosses, flat tires, bills, door-to-door salesmen, telemarketers, flu shots, spilled milk, coloring on the wall, a lost cat, and lightening scaring the dog... I think you get my point.

If a couple like that only considered themselves married because they "felt" married they would be in trouble. They have to look at the ring on their left hand and say, *"Yep, I must still be married because I still have the ring on."* They cannot afford to go by feelings and neither can we, especially when we are talking about the Secret Place.

God always makes a way

I know those who have young children, those who have jobs where you are always on call, and even those who are shift workers with two jobs, might be saying, *"How? How could I ever do what you are talking about?"* I really do know that frustration. When I was camp director for many years at our church it was common for our staff to work twelve to eighteen hours a day. We did this throughout the entire summer; Margie included. I was also the youth pastor at the same time preaching two services per week. Not to mention we had three kids and their activities, writing the daily devotions, pets, and everything else a family deals with.

But, just like Peter, we had to step out of our limitations and into the unlimited realm of Jesus. When he stepped out on that water, with no idea how he would walk on water, Peter accomplished the impossible as Jesus did His stuff. (Matt. 14:25-32) Even when Peter began to slip under the waves,

Jesus was there to rescue him and "walk with him" back to the boat. I don't think Jesus carried Peter back to the boat. I just can't picture that. I believe Jesus lifted him up and said, *"Come on Peter, this is how you do it."*

That same Jesus will help you with what seems to be an impossible schedule. When we dedicate our day to Him, it's amazing how He can make things go better so our time is multiplied. I have seen it happen in my own life time after time. Don't forget, you are meeting with the One who made the sun stand still so Joshua could have a few more hours to finish up a battle. (Josh. 10:13) I believe that same God will do what it takes for you to enjoy some alone time with Him.

You are called to fellowship with Jesus!

As a person becomes more and more disciplined in making the Secret Place a part of their life, they will certainly begin to see and experience the fruit of their labor. Once the Lord visits with you, and shares something out of His Word that "winds your clock," you will experience motivation like never before. When you see the goodness of God as it manifests right before you it only causes you to desire Him more and more. I don't really like to say it this way, but you can really get addicted to these special times with God. It's the only addiction that has great results.

Sometimes I may go several months without really feeling anything at all from my time in the Secret Place. But oh when He does give me something tangible. It will keep me going for another six months! I can only do what I do because of this REALationship with God. I am only alive because of a REALationship with God. And for me, the majority of this REALationship has been built in the Secret Place. Stay focused and you will stay motivated. God gives you a grace to fulfill what He has called you to. And He has called you to have fellowship with Jesus so you can be one with the Father. (1 Cor. 1:9) He will give you everything you need to do this. Trust Him.

"I hear you, but what if I fail?" How can you fail? A person only fails when they quit; when they give up. The Bible says in Psalms 34:19, *"Many are the afflictions of the righteous but the Lord delivers him out of them all."* All means all. If you are being afflicted with something then evidently God is not through because He said He would deliver you out of them ALL. The only thing that keeps God from doing His part is if we quit.

When I was suffering through those years of back pain, I wanted to quit almost daily. God kept reminding me He wasn't finished. I have no idea why it took sooooooooooo long. I just know He kept His Word. He finished and delivered me out of it ALL. He had told me there would be an end to the back pain and when it ended, the ministry He called me to would explode. That is exactly what happened. Don't let discouragement, depression, stress, grief, or anything else stop you from your FIRST calling. You are called to fellowship with Jesus.

A Secret Place Check List

As you can see, I really want to help you get into the Secret Place. To help you even more, here is a little check list I made for you.

1. Make the decision to dive into the Secret Place.

2. Get prepared by: setting your alarm, going to bed early enough to wake up when the alarm goes off, have your Bible, a journal, and something to write with. Perhaps have a Bible reading plan like the 32/11 one I suggested or however you want, but have something. No closing the eyes and pointing.

3. PRAY for the Holy Spirit to wake you up.

4. Have a "place" where it's quiet and secluded if possible. If not, get headphones and worship music.

5. When the alarm goes off, GET UP! No hitting the snooze button. Brush your teeth (I'm serious.) and dive in.

6. Journal about it. If you have nothing to write, don't be afraid to write that down. Write down that you didn't come to the Secret Place to "get something" but to "give" something. Eventually, you will have plenty to write in your journal.

7. Apply all of these tips and then reapply often.

There you go! Step by step, you are on your way! Obviously, I wrote this for those who want to get up early. If you choose a different time then tweak it to fit yourself. You will settle into your own plan soon enough. This is just a suggestion to get you started.

Need some more? Here is one more idea for you on "how" to apply what you have learned about the Secret Place. Read Matthew 6:6 which I talked about earlier in the book. Break it down word by word. With each word (or phrase) you read, stop, and DO what it says. When you finish do the same thing the next day. Do it every day and implement verses seven and eight. After a month or two of this, you are IN the Secret Place. Just like sunscreen, *"Apply and then reapply."* Simple.

Watch out for the "little foxes"

The Bible says we are not ignorant of the devil's tactics. (2 Cor. 2:11) One thing we must all realize, satan's number one goal is to keep you away from God. He doesn't want to deal with you once you have been in God's presence. So, it only makes sense that the Secret Place is an offense to the devil. The hardest fight in your life is the one that's fought for your time alone with God.

Everything from daily distractions to arguments to depression has been thrown at me at one time or another. We learn to guard our time with the Lord as a jeweler guards a precious diamond. The Secret Place is where we fellowship with the *"Pearl of great price"* (Matt. 13:46). Therefore, we must treat this quality time with God like a "pearl of great price." I pray I will hear my alarm. I set two if necessary. I do whatever it takes. I know I sound like a maniac but that is how serious this is for me.

I have experienced God's direction, deliverance, healing, motivation, rest, peace, souls saved, and a thousand other things while IN the Secret Place. With things like that coming out of my time with the Lord you can be sure I am going to protect and preserve it as much as possible. Of course, that doesn't mean I let all my responsibilities at home become neglected. I am just saying, it has to be a priority that we protect.

Ask the Holy Spirit to show you those *"little foxes that spoil the vine"* (Song of Sol. 2:15) otherwise known as time-wasters. I have followed little trails of what I "thought" was so important only to look back and see it was a time-waster sent by the devil. We have to learn to recognize these kinds of things and stop them before they happen. Don't let the enemy rob you of what God has called you to.

Passion in the midst of pain

I really do pray the Lord will give each of you reading this book a passion for the Secret Place. I pray you will experience His presence in a personal way unlike anything you have ever imagined. In other words, I pray you have a REALationship with the Lord. Jesus already paved the way, and with the help of the Holy Spirit, you can walk that path daily.

I guess one of the reasons I am so passionate about this whole subject is due to the "life" I have experienced from the Secret Place myself. I am not just talking about things IN life, I am talking about life itself; mainly my life.

As you have already read, I stepped out of the Secret Place on that Monday morning, July 5, 1993 only to step under a backhoe several hours later. As Psalms 91:14-16 says though, because we know His Name He will rescue us and give us long life. A lifestyle in the Secret Place, prayers of others, doctors and nurses who listened to God, and the grace and mercy of God saved my life that day. As you can imagine, I was convinced the Secret Place was a worthwhile venture.

Then years later, here came the fall down the stairs and well over five years of debilitating back pain. On came the effects of tons of pain medications, the effects of nonstop pain itself, and finally the staph infection in my spinal column; with no hope in sight. Once again, my wife heard the death-threat from satan towards her husband and I was faced with not seeing the fulfillment of what God has called me to do.

And… then came the BIGGER EFFECTS of the Secret Place. When I was given little hope, God gave me hope as I was alone with Him. He once again showed Himself alive to Margie and me. Life, life the way Jesus lives, made its way to me once again. The times in the Secret Place were becoming more valuable daily. As I have typed this entire book, I have done it completely and totally pain free from that back pain! Thank You, Jesus!

Experience the power which comes from a REALationship with God

However... don't you hate it when someone throws that word "however" in… it usually means, "Uh Oh." However, I am seeing the God who "sees in secret" do His thing once again. In 2008, I was having some issues with my hands. I thought it was carpal tunnel syndrome and ignored it. I was tired of going to doctors. This took place several months after my back surgery.

By a prompting from Margie, I went to the surgeon who had operated on my back so he could look at my hands. He sent me to a neurologist at a major hospital in the Houston, Texas Medical Center. They diagnosed me with ALS, also known as Lou Gehrig's Disease. The statistics show an average life span of only three to five years after diagnosis. Once again, I am thanking God that anything and everything is available in the Secret Place when you have a REALationship with Jesus Christ.

I don't know how people make it through the attacks of the enemy without a REALationship with Jesus. God has given me His promise of healing. He has even given me a born-again, Spirit-filled, Christian neurologist, who is in complete agreement with Margie and me for a miracle. The Lord has assured me I do not have to leave this earth before I can say, *"I have finished my course," (2 Tim. 4:7)* the way the apostle Paul did. And three to five years is certainly not enough time for me to finish my course so I am expecting to be satisfied with long life. (Ps. 91:16)

How can I deal with all these death threats? It's only by the grace God has provided through Jesus Christ. It's through Jesus I now have direct access to the Father. I am not talking about seeing Him as a person sees something in a museum. I am talking about being able to KNOW HIM PERSONALLY because of the high price Jesus paid. When we see Jesus, we see His Father. We become one with Him. Do you really think the devil can put death on the one who has become "one" with THE One? I don't think so.

We will all die eventually unless Jesus returns first. That does NOT mean we have to leave one day early though. Psalms 91:16 says God will satisfy the "Secret Place dweller" with LONG LIFE. I am so thankful I am a Secret Place dweller. Don't feel sorry for me... feel sorry for the devil. He has problems galore because of these "Secret Place" fanatics like YOU and me.

Oh, by the way, I just told you how this whole problem started in my hands. They became so weak it has been difficult to type among other things. I am talking about difficulty to the degree of oftentimes using one finger to type one letter at a time. Well, every one of the approximately 60,000 words in this book were typed with the two hands the devil tried to take from me; and I used all of my fingers! God's grace and mercy allowed me to type like a wild man as HE gave me the words. That poor devil; he seriously has troubles he does not know how to handle.

My lungs have shown unbelievable improvement since this latest diagnosis as well; which doctors say NEVER happens with a diagnosis of ALS. Ah yes, the God of the miraculous at His best, Doctor Jesus doing His thing. *"What about the devil?"* Yeah... that's still a problem... but NOT for me! Poor thing, he's an eternal loser and doesn't even know it. With Christ, WE are the winners! Our God is BIGGER than anything that comes against us. And when we are hanging out with Him, NOTHING is impossible! (Luke 1:37)

Patience and application

Patience will be your friend so embrace it. Remember it takes time to build a REALationship. This isn't some get-rich-scheme way of Christianity. This is a lifestyle change. It's something we will be building until we meet Jesus face to face. And even then, knowing God will still be an inexhaustible relationship that will take all of eternity to accomplish.

Be patient while spending time with the Lord. Don't try to rush this relationship. Enjoy the journey. Every moment you spend with the Lord will enhance your desire for more. There is no need for condemnation when you feel you missed the mark, so don't even go there. You are meeting with God, you know, the One who loves you unconditionally. Relax, be patient, and enjoy.

Application is everything. Once we have learned something it has to be applied. Without application, the truth revealed is only a memory. It's an unfinished journey. Jesus is the Alpha and the Omega, which means He is the beginning and the end. He is a finisher. And because of His example, we can be a finisher too. To be a finisher though there has to be a beginning, a starting point.

Take everything the Lord has shown you through this book and apply it to your life. Start somewhere, but start. Then, as you meet with Him, He will enlighten you and empower you for more. Take what He shows you and apply it to your life. This is a life long pattern for success. I don't mean man's definition of success; I am talking about success according to God. His success outshines our success by a long shot.

Closing words

Are you convinced yet of the value of a REALationship with God? If not, you only have a few more paragraphs with me. Here goes...

I know I am certainly not the only one who is passionate about my REALationship with God. I am not the only one who has written a book about the Secret Place. I am just "another one." I am another one who found the secret, which is no longer a secret. The only secret is what takes place inside the Secret Place. The Secret Place itself was never meant to be a secret at all. That's why Psalms 91 was written. That's also why Jesus talked about it and was the example for it.

Now, it's up to us to do something with it. I want to keep diving into more and more of God so He can continue revealing Himself to me. After each revelation from the Lord, I want to shout it from the rooftops that it's totally possible to KNOW God. I want to tell everyone I can that Jesus paid the price so we could come "boldly" before the throne room of God. (Heb. 4:16) We don't have to be afraid of Him. He is our Heavenly Father. It's a REALationship.

With the price Jesus paid, and with the help of the Holy Spirit, we can know our Father and be one with Him. It is the greatest privilege a person on earth could ever have offered to them. God has already initiated this relationship. He has already extended His hand through the extended hands of His

Son on the cross. God has already knocked on our door. The only thing He is waiting for is people like you and me to open that door. (Rev. 3:20)

So, I will ask you one more time. Are you ready to meet with the Lord on a regular basis, for the purpose of KNOWING Him? Are you ready to take your good relationship with God to a level beyond what you are already experiencing? Are you ready to see a relationship with God transform into a REALationship with Him? If so, that's awesome. If not, you will. The seed is planted. It's just a matter of time. Just remember, it's no longer a secret.

I have only one more thing to say. And that is, *"Put this book down and DIVE IN to a REALationship with God... in the Secret Place!"*

BIBLE STUDY QUESTIONS

I have included these Bible Study Questions for those of you who may be interested in sharing the message of this book with others. And really, the message of this book is all about THE Message in God's Book, the Bible. The message of the Secret Place transformed my life forever. I pray it has done the same for you. Now you have the opportunity to share YOUR experiences with those you know. Just think if all over the great world we live in people would dive into an intimate and personal REALationship with God. The results would be overwhelming for sure!

Here are a few tips that will help you with your Bible study group, cell group, Sunday school class, or whatever kind of gathering you lead or participate in.

1. Pray before each meeting.

2. Try to engage everyone in the group as you work your way through the study questions.

3. Do your best to keep one or two people from doing all the talking. You do this by saying, "Let's hear from someone who hasn't shared yet."

4. Every answer someone gives is important and it took courage for him or her to speak up in a group setting. So, make them great regardless of their answers or comments.

5. Don't be afraid of a little bit of silence. Let them think.

6. Try to stay focused on your topic. If it gets "off course," you can bring it back by saying, "Let's get back to our question we are trying to discuss right now which reads, _____."

7. Encourage personal experiences that are relevant to the topic.

8. Summarize what you have discussed during your time together so it stays in their heart.

9. Encourage the group to continue their commitment to get alone with God so they will enjoy a REALationship with Him.

10. Pray over what took place during your time together and pray for God's blessings on the peoples' lives.

Enjoy your time together and I always welcome any good reports from you or your group. E-mail me at: *Kevin@ PastorKevin.com.* For more information or for ideas for a LIVE appearance via the Internet or in person, feel free to contact me at: *281-235-8845* or on Skype with my username: *TheNetRev.* God Bless You!

CHAPTER I

RUN OVER BY A 13,000 LB TRACTOR; LENGTHWISE!

1. How does a life-threatening accident, diagnosis, or event change a person's life? If they are saved? If they are not saved?

2. When the tractor ran over Kevin, do you think it was God's will for his life?

3. How did the Secret Place affect Kevin in this accident?

4. Is it possible that Kevin's intimate relationship with God played a major part in his surviving this tragedy? Was it just a coincidence?

5. Would you agree that Kevin experienced a legitimate miracle?

6. Have you ever experienced a miracle?

CHAPTER 2

WHAT IS THIS SECRET PLACE?

1. Before reading this book had you ever heard of the Secret Place?

2. What is the meaning of the term "Secret Place?"

3. Is this Secret Place something for every Christian or just certain ones?

4. How can the Secret Place benefit me?

5. Do you have quality alone time with God in the Secret Place? How often?

6. Why do you think it's called a secret?

CHAPTER 3

IT ALL STARTED WITH A CROSSWALK

1. What is a crosswalk?

2. What do you think carrying a twelve-foot cross would do to you spiritually? Physically? Emotionally?

3. What was the life-changing event that happened during the journey? How did it change Kevin's life and ministry?

4. Can God take our mess-ups and turn them into victories?

5. What would you do if you saw someone carrying a cross down the road?

6. What other life-changing things can you learn from this unique journey?

CHAPTER 4

‒ ‒

WHAT'S A "HETTIE?"

1. What is a Hettie?

2. How did Hettie discover the Secret Place? Can you identify with Hettie's reason?

3. What is the one "key" that stands out the most from this encounter with Hettie?

4. Is your life an example someone can follow when it comes to having an intimate relationship with God?

5. How does the revelation of "observation" help you with your relationship with God? With others?

6. What do you want to be doing when you are eighty years old?

CHAPTER 5

-- --

THE TWO MOST IMPORTANT QUESTIONS
YOU WILL EVER ASK

1. What are the two most important questions?

2. Who should ask these questions?

3. How long does it take you to find the answers to these questions?

4. Why is it so important that you ask these questions in the same order that Paul (Saul) did?

5. How do these questions relate to the Secret Place?

6. Can you think of any other examples in the Bible where this "who before what" principle is used? What about in your own life?

C H A P T E R   6

EVERY CHRISTIAN'S GREATEST CALLING

1. What exactly IS a calling?

2. Is a calling the same as a purpose?

3. Does every Christian have a calling and if so, how can you find your calling?

4. Do you know your calling? If so, what is it? If not, what will you do to find out?

5. What can the Secret Place do to help you find your calling?

6. How will you know you actually heard from God and not the devil or yourself?

CHAPTER 7

KNOWING GOD VS. KNOWING "ABOUT" GOD

1. What is the difference between knowing about God and knowing God?

2. If God wants us to know him, why isn't it easier?

3. How in the world can a human being actually know such a Holy God?

4. What does the Bible say about Jesus knowing His Father, God?

5. How does spending time alone with God in the Secret Place help you to know God?

6. Where are you with these two things? Do you know God or just know "about" Him? Is there more to know?

CHAPTER 8

- -

PSALMS 91—HOW ONE CHAPTER
CHANGED MY LIFE

1. How can "dwelling in the Secret Place" as mentioned in the first verse, produce all those other good things in the rest of the chapter?

2. Psalms 91 is in the Old Testament; so, does it still apply to us in today's world?

3. What does it mean to "dwell" in the Secret Place?

4. Does Psalms 91 only help after-the-fact, for comfort and rescue, or will it actually *prevent* harm?

5. How does a person apply the promises in Psalms 91 to their life?

6. With so many benefits in Psalms 91 how do you stay focused on the "dwelling in the Secret Place" part?

CHAPTER 9

- -

DOES GOD REALLY WAKE UP AT 5:00 AM?

1. How can talking to God in the morning be any different than talking to Him at night?

2. What does the Bible have to say about getting up early to spend time with God?

3. Have you ever spent quality alone time with God early in the morning? Did it seem to help you in any way?

4. Are you convinced that having this time with God in the early morning is something you need to try? If so, what is your plan to do it?

5. What is God's outlook as to HIS reason for wanting to meet with us early in the morning?

6. Would you say this is a matter of "opinion" or is it an actual pattern in the Bible we would benefit from if we follow it?

CHAPTER 10

WHAT AM I SUPPOSED TO DO IN
THE SECRET PLACE?

1. What is the correct amount of time a person should spend in the Secret Place? How often?

2. How does a person get in the routine of spending time in the Secret Place without that time becoming routine?

3. What is the ultimate goal of spending time in the Secret Place?

4. How is spending time in the Secret Place different from reading the Bible and talking to God throughout your daily activities?

5. What can we see in the life of Jesus that reflects some sort of benefit from His time in the Secret Place?

6. What does a person DO while in the Secret Place?

CHAPTER II

THE LOST ART OF BEING STILL

1. What does it mean to be still? What's the point?

2. What does Psalms 46:10 mean to you?

3. Why is being still seen as a lost art?

4. How can someone afford the *luxury* of being still when there's so much to do and so little time to do it?

5. What is the importance of being still in conjunction with the Secret Place?

6. Is anything really happening when a person is "being still" in the Secret Place?

CHAPTER 12

CROSSING THE THRESHOLD

1. What does crossing the threshold mean?

2. What does crossing the threshold represent in a person's walk with God?

3. What, if anything, do you have to leave behind in order to cross the threshold?

4. What awaits a person on the other side of the threshold?

5. What is meant by the term, a "weighty bride?"

6. How will you know when you have crossed the threshold?

CHAPTER 13

BEHIND CLOSED DOORS

1. What do you think the meaning of the term, "Behind Closed Doors" signifies?

2. Discuss the different steps for our prayer time as mentioned in Matthew 6:6.

3. Specifically, what does "shutting the door," mean? What does it accomplish?

4. What goes on behind these closed doors?

5. Discuss what Jesus meant in Matthew 6:6 when He said, *"...your Father who sees in secret shall reward you openly."*

6. How can spending time alone with God produce spiritual disciples?

CHAPTER 14

-- --

JUMP-START YOUR JOURNAL

1. What is the difference between a diary and a journal?

2. What does writing in a journal do for your life?

3. How does writing in a journal keep you more focused on what God is speaking to you?

4. Why should I journal when I don't feel like God ever speaks to me? Will journaling change this?

5. What are some practical pointers of journaling that will help you to be successful at journaling?

6. What benefits will a person eventually see after many journal entries?

CHAPTER 15

DIVE IN!

1. What is the first crucial step in diving into the Secret Place?

2. How will you plan to make time for the Secret Place when you don't seem to have enough time as it is?

3. What is YOUR plan for time alone with God?

4. If you miss some of your times with God does this mean you have failed?

5. Name some specific ways you have benefitted from this book.

6. What is the number one thing that would try to distract you from diving into or staying in the Secret Place? What will you do to keep this from happening?

**Intermedia
Publishing Group**

Publishing That Works For You

Do you need a speaker?

Do you want Kevin Kinchen to speak to your group or event? Then contact Larry Davis at: (623) 337-8710 or email: ldavis@intermediapr.com or use the contact form at: www.intermediapr.com.

Whether you want to purchase bulk copies of *The Secret Place, Revealed* or buy another book for a friend, get it now at: www.imprbooks.com.

If you have a book that you would like to publish, contact Terry Whalin, Publisher, at Intermedia Publishing Group, (623) 337-8710 or email: twhalin@intermediapub.com or use the contact form at: www.intermediapub.com.